The Power of SMART Goals:

Using Goals to Improve Student Learning

By Jan O'Neill and Anne Conzemius

With Carol Commodore and Carol Pulsfus

Solution Tree

Cover Design by Grannan Graphic Design, Ltd.
Text Design and Composition by TG Design Group

Printed in the United States of America
ISBN 1-932127-87-9

Dedication

We dedicate this book to Ellen Johnston-Hale ("The Bubble Lady") and John B. Zimmerman.

—Jan O'Neill and Anne Conzemius

To all my students over the years, both young and old, who taught me about learning.

—Carol Commodore

To my husband, Dan, and my children, Richard, John, and Emily, who continually help clarify my thoughts and feelings about the power of learning.

—Carol Pulsfus

Acknowledgements

Authors just put words on paper. Practitioners—those who implement ideas every day in classrooms, schools, and districts—are the ones who do the real "heavy lifting." We have been honored to work with exceptional practitioners as we have sought to both capture what is working well with implementing SMART goals, and also to broaden and deepen that work beyond our previous two books. This book reflects a multitude of lifetimes; there are so many people who have influenced our thinking, supported our endeavors, and shaped our translation of their ideas and experiences into this book. Though we cannot possibly thank them all, we do want to acknowledge the unique and special contributions of a few.

First, the practical applications that are the backbone of *The Power of SMART Goals* came from our colleagues in the field, among them Sue Abplanalp, Bob Donaldson, Mary Bowen-Eggebraaten, Sandy Gunderson, Barb Hagens, Glen Jenkins, Ginny Kester, Jamie Lipovsky, Dennis Love, Laura Love, Paula Martin, Ellen Perconti, Jo Pirlott, Michele Sandro, Lori Storer, Bil Zahn, and the teams of people with whom they work. We also thank our active QLD network of consultants—Betty Burks, Carol Commodore, Linda D'Acquisto, Valerie Gregory, Barbara Hauser, Gwen Lee, Janet Malone, Carol Pulsfus, Christy Reveles, and Jo Seidel—for helping hone this work over the years. In addition, we want to acknowledge the many hours that Carol Pulsfus and Carol Commodore contributed to writing, revising, coordinating, and guiding the content and format of this book. Any errors are ours alone, and where content has been improved, we must thank the extensive list above.

Secondly, a special thanks to Michelle Larson who has been with us from the start. Michelle deserves special recognition *every day*—she is always one step ahead, anticipating client and organizational needs, and ready to lighten things up when we get too deep! To our trusted advisors and friends Bill Steinberg and Rich Teerlink, we always appreciate your unselfish gifts of time, listening, and an outside perspective. And to QLD Learning as a company, thank you for being willing to "give us up" (but not give up on us!) for months at a time.

We continue to be inspired and guided by the enduring great works of Linda Lambert, Peter Senge, Rick and Becky DuFour and Bob Eaker, Mike Schmoker, Michael Fullan, Parker Palmer, Stephen Covey, Bruce Wellman, Laura Lipton, Rick Stiggins, Bob Marzano, and Fred Newmann. We hope our work honors yours, and complements and extends it as well.

To our friends at Solution Tree, it has been a pleasure once again working with such a delightfully supportive, caring, and thoughtful publishing team. Thanks especially to Rhonda Rieseberg, Suzanne Kraszewski, Jane St. John, and Shannon Ritz, and to Jeff Jones for once again signing on with us for the ride.

Finally, we must acknowledge that although putting ideas into words and onto paper may seem a relatively simple, straightforward task, the creative process that occurs before, during, and after knows no boundaries of time or place. When we write, we live the work, which means that our families must live the work with us— sometimes not by choice. Hank, Bill, and Luke: You went on this journey again with us and never once complained. You have contributed in so many ways, not the least of which has been the sacrifice of family time. We could not have done this without your patient understanding and support. Will you take us back now?

—Jan O'Neill and Anne Conzemius
Madison, Wisconsin

Table of Contents

Figures, Features, and Reflections

Figures

Features

Reflections

About the Authors

Jan O'Neill, M.S.

Jan O'Neill has been an educator for more than 25 years, amassing diverse experience at the preschool, primary, intermediate, and middle school levels. As a teacher-leader, she served on district K–12 curriculum committees and developed language arts curricula for middle school. Leaving education to earn a master's degree in public policy and administration from the University of Wisconsin LaFollette Institute, Jan studied with Dr. Deming and others involved in the quality movement, and she became one of the pioneers in applying continuous improvement principles system-wide in government and healthcare. After consulting with the private sector for 7 years, Jan returned to education to establish QLD Learning with Anne Conzemius. Her work has been published in local, state, and national newsletters and journals. In addition to *The Power of SMART Goals*, Jan is coauthor with Anne Conzemius of *The Handbook for SMART School Teams* (Solution Tree [formerly National Educational Service], 2002) and *Building Shared Responsibility for Student Learning* (ASCD, 2001).

Anne Conzemius, M.S.

Anne Conzemius brings a broad range of experience to her practice. Prior to establishing QLD Learning with her partner, Jan O'Neill, Anne served as assistant state superintendent for Wisconsin's Department of Public Instruction. From 1988 to 1990, she served as director of employee development and training for the state of Wisconsin. She worked in public schools for 8 years as a school psychologist. She later consulted in the private sector, bringing continuous improvement principles and methods to a variety of businesses and industries. Her work has been published in local, state, and national educational newsletters and journals. In addition to *The Power of SMART Goals*, Anne is coauthor with Jan O'Neill of *The Handbook for SMART School Teams* (Solution Tree [formerly National Educational Service], 2002) and *Building Shared Responsibility for Student Learning* (ASCD, 2001). Anne holds two master's degrees from the University of Wisconsin-Madison, one in educational psychology and one in industrial relations.

Carol Commodore, Ed.D.

Carol Commodore was a classroom teacher for more than 20 years. She has also held positions as assistant superintendent and administrator for assessment. Today Carol is a founding member of Leadership, Learning and Assessment, LLC, and a professional development associate of Rick Stiggins' Assessment Training Institute. Carol strongly believes in bringing students into the decision-making and implementation processes of assessment and instruction. She is continually looking for meaningful ways to assist educators in developing reflective tools that will bring insight and joy to them and their students in the educational process. Carol's work takes her across the United States, Canada, Europe, Asia, and the Middle East.

Carol received her bachelor's degree in Spanish and English from Dominican College in Racine, Wisconsin, her master's degree in curriculum and supervision from the University of Wisconsin-Milwaukee, and her doctoral degree in leadership for the advancement of learning and service from Cardinal Stritch University in Milwaukee, Wisconsin. Her dissertation is titled "The Impact of Assessment on Learners and Their Learning."

Carol Pulsfus, M.S.

Carol Pulsfus is a consultant for multiple organizations and agencies including QLD Learning, About Learning, Inc., CESA 5, and Red Pine Consultants Group. She has been facilitating successful 4MAT System seminars for over 12 years and is building facilitation skills for a repertoire of new seminars as research emerges in the field. Carol's 31 years in education includes being a teacher at all grade levels, an elementary school principal, a professional development coordinator, and an adjunct professor for Viterbo College and for the University of Wisconsin-Platteville in the Department of Teaching and Learning.

Carol's certification is in elementary education. She has a master's degree in educational administration from the University of Wisconsin-Whitewater. In 2000, she received the Educational Influence Award from the Wisconsin Association for Supervision and Curriculum Development. She has written and coordinated multiple Comprehensive School Reform Demonstration (CSRD) grants in Wisconsin. Through CSRD, she has mentored school districts and organizations for many years, validating long-term, systematic professional development. Carol also works in the private sector, focusing on strategic planning, leadership, and management issues.

Foreword

By Mike Schmoker

Many have written about the supreme importance of goals. But in this excellent book, *The Power of SMART Goals*, Jan O'Neill and Anne Conzemius have done something original and important: They have helped us see that goals are a useful and powerful prism through which we can see the totality of school improvement. Goals, rightly understood, both urge and unify the most vital elements of school success. Through this prism, O'Neill and Conzemius allow us to see, with great clarity, the significant and manifold implications of getting goals right—and the needlessly destructive consequences of getting them wrong.

The Power of SMART Goals helps to clarify the fact that first and foremost, goals redefine our relationship to work and effort. In turn, SMART goals redefine the relationship between effort and personal satisfaction. What the authors call "joy in work" can only be experienced when daily work is linked to goals that allow us to see that our thoughts and efforts connect, at every moment, to something larger and worthwhile—to something we can see and examine and enjoy. Without this orientation, effort and energy can only dissipate into aimless, joyless toil. Without goals, we will never work as hard or as smart to accomplish what is important—to us, and for our students.

Mike Schmoker is the author of *RESULTS* (ASCD, 1999) and *The RESULTS Fieldbook* (ASCD, 2001). His forthcoming book is *The Opportunity: From Brutal Facts to the Best Schools We've Ever Had* (ASCD, in press).

This book also advances our understanding of how goals have the power to help us *prioritize*: to prevent the unfocused, time-wasting folly of so much that goes on in the name of school improvement. As the authors point out, SMART goals are notoriously absent in most of these plans. And so, once written, they are typically "forgotten . . . until the next plan is due." Thus they exert little or no influence on student learning. Rather than focus, as the authors urge, on the "vital few" elements and actions that promote better instruction, the "goals" that fill the typical improvement plan only seduce us into confusing action with outcomes, good intentions with results. Nothing could be worse for schools or those who work and learn in them.

The perfect example of this confusion can be seen in how we confuse goals with training—the common, garden-variety professional development that the authors ingeniously refer to as "adult pull-out programs." These always sound great, but too often constitute a kind of bland, superficially appealing "menu" with something for everyone, regardless of any connection to SMART goals. The items on this menu are seldom carefully selected (or *rejected*) on the basis of their ability to clearly advance teams and individuals toward the achievement of clear, measurable progress toward substantive learning.

This book will persuade you that goals, rightly rendered, can be seen as far more than a component of improvement; they are in fact the glue that holds teams and their efforts together against the incessant distractions that bombard us at every turn. They screen out the competing demands that cause teams to lose focus and thus waste precious time, thought, and energy. SMART goals—whether short-term or long-term—focus our attention on the simplest and most vital elements of improvement, like formative assessment results, which directly connect to goals and without which we cannot see or enjoy our progress. Only effective goals demand such attention to measurable short-term results that sustain and nourish the momentum that Jim Collins (and many others, in so many words) tell us is the soul of improvement.

O'Neill and Conzemius argue, quite compellingly, that goals are the common denominator—at all levels. Logically enough, they are just as emphatic about the importance of helping students themselves to be goal-oriented, so that they can see and enjoy their own palpable progress and accomplishments regularly and frequently, along with those areas where they can be better. Of course student goals, like all SMART goals, thrive on frequent feedback. The authors help us see that we have only scratched the surface of helping students work deliberately and optimistically toward their own "I can" goals, as they begin to realize that *they are far smarter than they think*. It's all about hope: the belief that hard, persistent effort will pay off. And as O'Neill and Conzemius assert, with such goal-oriented structures, "Hope can be learned."

Effective goals urge us to attend to the most critical elements of improvement: solid evidence of learning, short-term results, common formative assessment (which reveals those short-term results), recognition and celebration of short-term results, and the all-important opportunity for teachers and students to enjoy— to "take joy"—in their work. These are the major, protean elements of substantive improvement.

Perhaps the primary theme of this book is that we cannot take these elements for granted. O'Neill and Conzemius are right: SMART goals—*rightly understood*—are still all too rare. Make no mistake: Such goals represent, in the authors' words, "business as *un*usual." This book makes a rich contribution to clarity about this most pervasive and practical concept, and helps us to understand and implement the goal-oriented principles and practices that will help schools to be vastly better than they are, vastly better than they ever thought they could be.

Chapter 1

Introduction:
The SMART Goals Process

"Would you tell me, please, which way I ought to go from here?" asked Alice.

"That depends a good deal on where you want to get to," said the Cat.

"I don't much care where—" said Alice.

"Then it doesn't matter which way you go," said the Cat.

—Lewis Carroll
From *Alice's Adventures in Wonderland* (2002, p. 53)

Think back to a time when you made a significant change in your life. Perhaps you were dissatisfied with your career or job, and so you pursued more education, a new position, or a different work setting. If you wanted to master a new hobby or sport, you may have enrolled in classes, joined a team, or sought personal coaching. Maybe you were unhappy about your weight, so you started a weight-loss program. Regardless of whether you were pursuing a dream of something better because you were unhappy or because you simply wanted something different, you probably set some goals toward accomplishing that dream and pursued those goals with passion, rigor, and perhaps even specificity: "I'll get a master's degree in educational psychology within 2 years," "I will be able to kayak grade-3 rapids by the time I'm 40," or "I'm going to lose 15 pounds by the end of the year."

Although most of us acknowledge the power of goals in our own lives, they remain the single most underestimated and under-utilized means of improving student learning—particularly in the classroom—in education today. In his meta-analysis of what works in schools, Marzano (2003) found that the impact on student achievement of setting instructional goals ranges from a low of 18 percentile points to a high of 41 percentile points. This means that if a student who starts at the 50th percentile has a teacher who sets clear instructional goals, that student could achieve anywhere from the 68th to the 91st percentile. With results as significant as this, it seems that more schools would be implementing goal-setting as a standard practice in their classrooms. Mike Schmoker (1999), in his bestseller *Results: The Key to Continuous School Improvement*, discusses 50 cases of schools and districts that are successfully applying a combination of goal-setting, teamwork, and data to improve student performance. However, in our experience, this is still not a widespread practice in schools today.

In our field research, we also discovered very few instances of *student* goal-setting, although in a meta-analysis of over 11,000 statistical factors conducted by Wang, Haertel, and Walberg (1994), the power of student engagement in setting and monitoring goals was found to be second only to active participation in impacting student learning. Some of the most powerful research on student goal-setting comes from the studies conducted on formative assessment by Black and Wiliam. They conclude from their meta-analysis of more than 20 studies that student-involved formative assessment produces "significant and often substantial learning gains" (1998, p. 140). The gains are particularly apparent for low achievers. In their seminal work "Inside the Black Box," the researchers write:

"When anyone is trying to learn, feedback about the effort has three elements: recognition of the *desired goal*, evidence about *present position*, and some understanding of a *way to close the gap* between the two." (1998, p. 143)

Although we found some powerful examples of students setting and monitoring their learning goals, these instances are still rare—in spite of the evidence of the impact it has on student achievement.

In 1991, Susan Rosenholz, the guru of goal-setting, found that most schools did not have clear, common goals. Mike Schmoker (1999), commenting on her work, writes:

"The existence of common goals in schools was . . . rare, and the lack of agreed-upon goals makes schools unique among organizations. She found that there was very little goal consensus—a collective agreement about what to work toward— even though her studies revealed that this element was the heart of what accounted for progress and success." (p. 25)

Today we find that many schools do have improvement goals, but they are all too often written into a mandated school improvement plan, submitted to the district, and then soon forgotten as everyone returns to "business as usual." The improvement goals do not drive the behavior of everyone in the school, and they are for the most part forgotten until the next plan is due. Because school goals are not being used to prioritize efforts and resources, which in turn focuses behavior, people naturally return to the daily list of urgent problems, issues, crises, and new initiatives, ending each day feeling overwhelmed by the sheer volume of activities. Even in those schools that have developed school improvement goals to focus their work as a school, goal-setting is rarely used at the classroom level to improve rates of learning, even though Schmoker calls these shorter-term goals "breakthrough" in nature because they are so powerful in improving achievement. As organizational development researchers Katzenbach and Smith (1993) write, "The attainability of specific performance goals helps teams maintain their focus on getting results" (p. 54). Great opportunities for improvement are being lost if teams of teachers are not using specific goals on a regular basis.

Individual Reflection: Business as Usual

To understand how easy it is to fall back into a routine of business as usual, try this kinesthetic exercise. Fold your hands the way you normally do. Notice which thumb is on top. Now refold your hands with the opposite thumb on top. How does that feel? Pretty uncomfortable, right? Now go back to the familiar way. Feels pretty good! But which way are you more aware of the position of your fingers? Probably the new way. The old way is business as usual; the new way is your learning edge, the place where you are more conscious, aware, and intentional. Our tendency is to unconsciously return to what is comfortable, but the "discomfort zone" is where we are most alert and focused. Goal-setting requires intentionality and purpose. It is not business as usual; in fact, it is just the opposite—it is business as <u>un</u>usual.

Goal-setting has yet to become personal, real, and compelling for us in our daily lives in school. As a result, we are missing one of the most powerful tools for helping all students achieve. The loss to adults is just as profound: We are missing opportunities to experience empowerment, efficacy, and what the late Dr. W. E. Deming called "joy in work." When collectively we share responsibility for goals, the synergy is palpable and self-renewing. There is a focused energy that connects us to each other, motivating us to try harder, to go further than we might have gone alone. Schools in which administrators, staff, students, and parents are engaged in goal-setting reap rewards more quickly and are able to sustain continuous improvement of results over time. There are many examples of this in our first book, *Building Shared Responsibility for Student Learning* (ASCD, 2001); in Mike Schmoker's book *Results: The Key to Continuous School Improvement* (ASCD, 1999); and in Richard Dufour, Robert Eaker, and Rebecca DuFour's books on professional learning communities, as well as in the research conducted by Emily Calhoun, Gordon Cawelti, Susan J. Rosenholz, and many others. These works are cited at the end of this book, and real-life case studies from different schools are included in chapter 7.

> ### Team or Individual Reflection: A Picture of Energy
> *Imagine a time when you were on a successful team, perhaps at work, in sports, or in the community. Recall the energy in the group, the sense of, "We're all in this together; we can do this." What would a picture of that energy look like? What would be a good metaphor for this energy? This is the kind of energy you can feel in a school where all are focused on the common goal of improving student learning, with the ultimate vision of ensuring that each and every student succeeds.*

Barriers to Goal-Setting and Monitoring

Hard Work

So why do we not use goal-setting and monitoring more pervasively as an improvement method in our schools? Certainly, one big reason is that adopting a goal-conscious state of mind is hard work. It takes time to develop real and compelling goals, and it is even more difficult to make time to continuously monitor progress on goals and then adjust our practices and programs accordingly. Given the current state of most schools where the daily "fires" are attended to and the longer-term "smoldering embers" remain neglected, we are simply not accustomed to a goal-setting habit of mind. The irony is that by investing in goal-setting and monitoring, we could reduce the number of problems that need attention. How many of those problems are actually caused by an underlying pattern of issues that are never deeply addressed and resolved? Are we really dealing with individual fires, each one independent and different from the others—or is it actually a *system* of fires? By focusing on just a critical few areas for improvement at a time, we could begin to answer these questions.

Lack of Common Assessments

Another reason we have neglected goal-setting and monitoring is that we have lacked curriculum-embedded classroom-based measures that we can examine collaboratively and systematically, that give us ongoing feedback about student learning and the effects of our instruction. Schools have traditionally left classroom assessment up to individual teachers, and as teachers, we are very comfortable with our own assessments, typically relying on unit tests, quizzes, worksheets, essays, and other means of testing our *own* students' knowledge. But until recently, with the rapid growth of the professional learning communities movement, we have rarely *co*developed assessments with our colleagues to assess learning for *our* collectively shared students. Without that built-in accountability and sense of shared responsibility, there is little that compels us to ask how *we* might be able to do better. Mike Schmoker (1999) speaks convincingly of the power of collectively analyzing student performance data when he writes:

> "Data can help us confront what we may wish to avoid and what is difficult to perceive, trace, or gauge: data can substantiate theories, inform decisions, impel action, marshal support, thwart misperceptions and unwarranted optimism, maintain focus and goal-orientation, and capture and sustain collective energy and momentum." (p. 49)

When common assessments include rubrics and criteria that clearly describe quality work, both teachers and students benefit from the analysis and the opportunity for specific corrective action. When teachers look at this performance data as a team, we can bring our theories together and generate many more options for improvement. When we look solely at our individual classroom's performance, we are left with only our own theories and solutions. In sum, the lack of common assessments keeps us practicing in isolation, preventing us from tapping into the full horsepower that a team with common purposes and measures would have.

Lack of Feedback

We are only now becoming familiar with the power of feedback, a key feature of the effective use of goals. Marzano (2003) reports that the impact of effective feedback on student achievement ranges from a low of 21 percentile points to a high of 41 percentile points. He notes, "Academic achievement in classes where effective feedback is provided to students is considerably higher than the achievement in classes where it is not" (p. 37). To gain this level of impact, the feedback must be timely, specific, and ongoing (formative assessment), versus only at the end of learning (summative assessment). Rick Stiggins calls this type of feedback "assessment *for* learning." Assessment *for* learning is a process of engaging students in understanding clear learning targets, using formative assessments for self-assessment and teacher feedback, and positioning learning in a nonjudgmental environment. When common assessments, collaboratively developed by teams of teachers, are used both formatively (during learning, to promote learning) and summatively (at the end of learning, to evaluate learning), teachers get the added benefit of promoting student learning as well as their own learning. In our experience, many schools are just beginning to recognize the combined power of formative and summative assessments.

Vulnerability

A final reason we do not use goal-setting and monitoring may be because it makes us feel vulnerable, pushing our "competency buttons"—those triggers that get pressed when we feel our skills are in question. As Rick Stiggins (2001) writes:

> "To the extent that you are clear and specific about the outcomes that you take on as your individual responsibility, you open yourself up to the possibility that some of your students may not be able

to hit the target after instruction and there will exist concrete, irrefutable assessment evidence of this." (p. 62)

When we develop goals as a team and agree to use common assessments, we are exposing ourselves not only to our students and our supervisors, but to our colleagues as well, which is perhaps even more challenging for many teachers. Teachers may feel a variation of test anxiety: When we are unsure of our skills, we worry about having others see what we do not know. Alternatively, traditional school cultures have not celebrated high-achieving teachers; in fact, many teachers are uncomfortable sharing their successes with their colleagues for fear they will be branded as "apple polishers" or worse. (Ironically, we seem to mirror the very behavior our students worry about!)

Yet another reason for a lack of goal-setting and monitoring is that if we have experienced nothing but shame and blame for our data, we will be much less inclined to set challenging improvement goals and want to monitor achievement on those goals. When teachers have seen nothing but poor results, and yet are working very hard, they lose confidence in their ability to affect student learning. They may have even come to believe that improved achievement just "can't happen with these kids" or that "our kids are different."

The Power of Results Thinking

Peter Senge (1990), in his classic work *The Fifth Discipline*, describes five disciplines of the learning organization, the first of which is "personal mastery." Senge writes, "Organizations learn only through individuals who learn. Individual learning does not guarantee organizational learning. But without it no organizational learning occurs" (p. 139). Personal mastery, Senge writes, "means approaching one's life as a creative work, living life from a creative as opposed to reactive viewpoint" (p. 141). Those with high levels of personal mastery regularly spend time reflecting on their vision, skills, and practices. They clarify what is important to them, and are clear about the current reality. They are extremely focused, but in a very particular way: "They *focus on the desired result itself*, not the 'process' or the means they assume necessary to achieve that result" (p. 164).

If we are truly going to transform our schools into places where each and every student is meeting and exceeding standards, we will first need to shift our thinking to focus on the results we want, a concept that is quite foreign for most educators. Schmoker (1999) claims, "We still do not give results the central concern they deserve. . . . We talk as though we want results, but we generally fail to make the kind of systematic, organized effort that produces them" (p. 3). In our business-as-usual mode, we tend to focus on the strategies, programs, activities, and innovations that we hope will lead to improved results.

Process Goals Versus Results Goals

In New Berlin High School, the improvement goal was "to integrate the math and science curriculum." Teachers had been implementing this curriculum for several years when they were asked, "So what has been the result of this integration?" The team answered, "The students are enjoying math and science more," and "As teachers we're enjoying being able to plan and teach together." The questioners persisted: "That's terrific, but what was the original purpose for the integration?" The teachers thought about it for a moment and then responded, "To reduce ninth-grade failure in math and science." "Has that happened?" they were asked. After quite a few moments, they said quietly, "We don't know." As a result of this conversation, the teachers were compelled to examine student performance data: grades and test scores. They found out that the failure rate was about the same as it had been several years ago—over 30%. After they got over their original disappointment, they went back to the drawing board to analyze why the integrated curriculum was not working as well as they had hoped. One of their discoveries was that students were not being identified early enough to be given the additional support they needed to be successful. Today the student failure rate is down to less than 10%.

As teachers, we have been taught to pay attention to planning our lessons, trying different strategies to engage different kinds of learners, identifying the scope and sequence of our curriculum, and deciding how we will evaluate student understanding of the content so that we can record grades. We are very comfortable focusing on *teaching*, but we have not been very focused on whether students have *learned*. As Rick DuFour says, the motto seems to have been, "I teach, I test, I hope for the best."

A focus on results is not just about test scores, however. A results focus means asking, "What do we want to achieve?" and "What are the outcomes we're shooting for?" at least as often as we ask, "What strategies should we try?" When we do not have a results-focus, we have a tendency to keep adopting new programs and initiatives, never stopping to ask about the outcomes we are seeking to achieve. Often these initiatives get masked in goal language although they are "process" goals. Process goals are limited in their effectiveness, since they only reference activities, programs, resources, or strategies—the things we will *do*, not the desired learning *result* of all that "doing." Unfortunately, the effect is intense busyness with very little progress. The good news is that, thanks in large part to the work of Schmoker and DuFour, Eaker, and DuFour, many more schools are now focused on improving results, and are no longer allowing "hope for the best" to be the prevailing view.

"The litmus test for a good school is not its innovations but rather the solid, purposeful, enduring results it tries to obtain for its students."

—Carl Glickman (1993, p. 50)

Our ability to focus on results is directly related to our individual orientation toward life itself. If we believe that others control us, that we have little power or freedom of movement, we will tend to simply react to life's challenges and opportunities, allowing ourselves to tumble and roll in its breakers, as if we were shells being pummeled on a beach. On the other hand, if we build in time to reflect on where we want to be, where we are now, and how we are going to close the gap between the two, we are energized, and we act proactively with choice and intentionality.

> ### Individual Reflection: Achieving Your Goal
>
> *Think about a personal goal you have in your life. Why do you want to pursue this goal? Are you unhappy with your current situation, or are you excited by the possibilities of something new and different? What will it look like, feel like, sound like, even taste like when you have achieved your goal? Imaging is a critical ingredient of "whole brain thinking." Record and/or draw some metaphors to show what it will be like when you have achieved your goal. Before you think about what you are doing to achieve your goal, take time to write your goal with a results orientation.*

The QLD Framework

When we first began working with schools in 1997, we developed an easy-to-remember framework to help clients keep the big picture in mind regardless of whether they were working in a small team, a school, a district, or an entire school community. This framework (figure 1.1) is a triangle—nature's most stable shape.

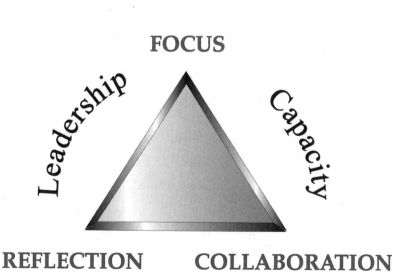

Figure 1.1: The QLD Framework for Shared Responsibility

At the top of the triangle is FOCUS, which means many things: having a clear vision about where you want to be; being true to your purpose and core values; always asking of every activity and plan, "How is this going to help students learn?"; and having the perseverance to never give up on a student. Focus is also about establishing clear, measurable, results-based goals—goals that are SMART.

In the left corner of the triangle is REFLECTION. This, too, means many things: the ability to pause, assess, and reflect on where one is; the data (quantitative, qualitative, intuitive) one looks at when seeking to make improvements; and the many forms of assessment that can be used to inform instructional practice; to provide feedback to students, parents, the school, and the community; and to evaluate program effectiveness.

In the right corner is COLLABORATION. Collaboration means the skills required to be an effective team; time for teaming; and partnerships between students, teachers, parents, the school, and the community. Collaboration also includes the action plans and strategies that accompany goals, as well as trust and a sense of "we're all in this together."

Finally, LEADERSHIP CAPACITY surrounds the triangle because when we focus collaboratively on data by setting and monitoring goals together, we grow our capacity to share responsibility for improving student learning. Linda Lambert (2003) writes, "Leadership capacity can refer to an organization's capacity to lead itself and to sustain that effort when key individuals leave" (p. 4). Leadership capacity is not only those skills and attitudes we develop—teaming, reflective inquiry, dialogue, collective responsibility—but it is also the various team *structures* created to pull all of us into the act of leadership. Lambert describes leadership capacity as both deep skillfulness in leadership and broad participation in leadership. "All" includes students, parents, staff, faculty, administrators, and community members. Structures include governance teams, learning teams, action teams, improvement teams, and so on. As leadership capacity grows, the culture of the school becomes more and more aligned with professional learning community (PLC) principles, and the key challenge moves from growing capacity to sustaining that capacity even as teachers, administrators, parents, and students leave.

Professional Learning Communities

Professional Learning Communities (PLCs) are schools that have embraced the principles of a learning organization through engaging multiple stakeholders in the development of shared vision, mission, values, and goals. PLCs are schools where there is a strong infrastructure of teams focused on improving student learning through ongoing collection and analysis of many different types of data. Schools that have developed themselves as strong PLCs are resilient in times of change because they never stop learning, changing, and improving.

The Power of SMART Goals

If you search the internet for "SMART goals," you will get more than one million results. The term "SMART goals" has been around for a long time, used by motivational speakers, exercise and fitness gurus, and corporate trainers and planners. The definitions of S-M-A-R-T vary, but most focus on specific, measurable, achievable goals that have a particular time frame. Users of SMART goals claim benefits ranging from financial security to achieving career dreams to lifetime happiness and inner peace. SMART goals have been in use by other industries for more than 20 years, but they are only now beginning to be valued in school settings.

S = Strategic and Specific

M = Measurable

A = Attainable

R = Results-based

T = Time-bound

We have been teaching SMART goals as a process since 1997, when we first began working with the New Berlin School District near Milwaukee, Wisconsin, to help their schools focus on improving results, not just processes. We began using the term "SMART" to describe the process for goal-setting. We define the acronym as "Strategic AND Specific, Measurable, Attainable, Results-based, and Time-bound." Each part of this definition is critical to student success.

Strategic

Why strategic? We ask schools to focus on just the "vital few" with their SMART goals. The vital few are high-leverage areas where the largest gaps between vision and current reality exist, and therefore the greatest gains will be seen. The Pareto Principle, first developed by Vilfredo Pareto at the turn of the century to describe the distribution of wealth (20% of the people owned 80% of the wealth), was adapted by Dr. Joseph Juran in the 1980s during the Quality Movement to describe the phenomenon of improvements occurring across the board when just a few problems are focused on. Juran was the first to write about the importance of focusing on the "vital few" to take care of the "essential many." Douglas Reeves' 90-90-90 research is an example of the Pareto Principle in action. In studying schools with 90% or more poverty, 90% or more minorities, and 90% or higher achievement, he discovered that many of these schools were focusing on writing across the curriculum (Reeves, 2000). As a result of their unrelenting attention to this critical thinking skill, students improved in other disciplines as well.

We also encourage schools and teams of teachers to think strategically by aligning their goals as a system. If the district's long-term goal is to ensure that all students are reading on grade level by the end of third grade, and reading is a great area of need for a school, then the building improvement goal should focus on reading, as should the collaborative classroom goals. With this type of alignment, resources and attention will be especially driven toward improvement of reading, and student learning in reading will dramatically improve—and improvements will be seen across all subjects.

Specific

Why specific? Specificity provides the concrete, tangible evidence of improvement that teams need to stay motivated. In being specific about goals, teams have clearer communication and more constructive conflict because they can focus on how to pursue the goals or how to change (Katzenbach & Smith, 1993). We encourage schools and teacher teams to focus on specific targets for improvement. They do this through the skills and learning targets on which they focus by targeting specific groups of students. Some students may just need additional test-taking strategies. Others may need more intensive instruction and time, while still others may have mastered the material and are ready to move on. By targeting students and skills, teachers become very focused in their approaches, and students benefit greatly from this more individualized approach.

Measurable

Measurability of a goal is critical, as we tend to focus our efforts on what gets measured. The tree diagram graphic organizer (see page 18) encourages schools and teachers to think in terms of multiple measures for each goal. School goals should focus primarily on summative measures, while classroom-level goals should be both summative and formative in their focus. The school community will want to review their measures one or more times a year to see if they are on track. Teachers will want more frequent, ongoing reviews of how students are performing on classroom-based measures both to assess learning and provide feedback and also to evaluate what was learned at the end of a quarter, semester, or year. Schools use the data to adjust resources, programs, schedules, staffing, and so on, while teachers use the data to improve their practice, provide feedback to students on their learning, and to summatively record student mastery. By using multiple measures, we get a more complete picture of learning, both in terms of benchmarks achieved and progress along the way.

Attainable

Goals need to be attainable, and also, as Goran Carstedt, the former head of IKEA Europe says, "People need goals worthy of their commitment." In other words, goals that motivate us to strive higher are those that are almost but not quite within our reach, that we need to stretch to achieve. Once achieved, our sense of satisfaction is far greater than if we had aimed low and got there. Attainability is very much correlated with how large the gap is that we want to close and how much focus, energy, time, and resources we are prepared to put into attaining the goal. These questions can best be addressed through data conversations in which teachers engage in collective inquiry and dialogue about how far they plan to go together.

"Learning goals give meaning to and act as a healthy check on the traditionally untethered tendency for public institutions to be satisfied with processes, regardless of outcomes."

—Mike Schmoker (1999, p. 30)

Results-Based

Results-based goals are motivating. We learn more through results-based goals because we have concrete benchmarks against which to measure our efforts. Process goals, such as implementing a new program or delivering a workshop, are simply not as motivating. We can check process goals off our lists and move on. The key question remains: "So what?" What improved? Did student learning improve as a result of what we did? Did teacher learning improve, which in turn improved student learning? When we ground goals in results, we build in immediate feedback that supports our sense of efficacy. When we achieve these goals, we feel proud of our accomplishments and want to do more, strive further. When we do not achieve the results we want, we can then go back to the drawing board and ask why. Was it in the implementation? The design? The evaluation? Were other factors involved? Should we try again, perhaps with a new plan?

Time-Bound

Finally, setting a time-bound goal—one that has a specific time frame—is critical. If you were to set a goal for yourself of running a mile in 8 minutes, but never set a time frame within which to achieve this goal, you could keep putting it off, not applying yourself to the task, and never reach your goal. On the other hand, if you were to say you would run that 8-minute mile by the end of summer, you would be motivated to get in shape, and you would hold yourself accountable to measuring your times. If you did not meet your goal within that time frame, then you would have an opportunity to learn why you did not and make adjustments. Setting a goal that is time-bound builds internal accountability and commitment.

> ## Individual Reflection: A SMARTer Goal
> *Return to your personal goal. Can you make your goal SMARTer? Apply the SMART criteria to your goal. How do you feel about your goal now? Has your motivation for achieving it increased?*

A Powerful Graphic Organizer for Creating SMART Goals

You probably use graphic organizers every day of your life—calendars, planners, PDAs, and agendas are all examples of these types of tools. Graphic organizers help us organize our thinking, create and monitor plans, connect isolated pieces of knowledge, and make meaning. In addition, graphic organizers are especially powerful when used by teams because they help distribute everyone's individual knowledge, making thinking visible by creating a powerful picture of what we are all thinking together. When we first worked with the New Berlin schools in 1997, we taught a very simple graphic organizer adapted from the "quality toolbox" called the tree diagram (figure 1.2). The school improvement teams began using the tree diagram to construct SMART goals and discovered that their collaboration became much more focused and concrete. In essence, the tree diagram helps makes goals SMARTer.

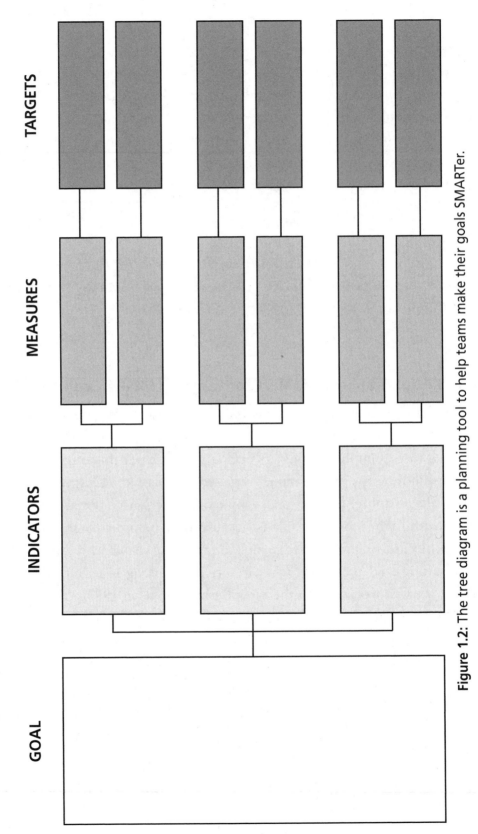

Figure 1.2: The tree diagram is a planning tool to help teams make their goals SMARTer.

The Goal

We will walk through the tree diagram's components from left to right, using a school academic goal as an example. The largest box at the far left is where you would put a results-based goal focused on the greatest area of need (what we also call "GAN"), the overall amount of improvement desired, and the time frame (figure 1.3). Since SMART goals close the gaps toward the long-term vision of all students meeting or exceeding standards, you will need to examine your data first to see what would be attainable and a goal worthy of commitment within a given time frame. We encourage schools to set goals that are at least 2 to 3 years out to give themselves the kind of longer-term strategic focus that would result in significant improvement.

GOAL

> 85% of students will be proficient writers at their grade level within 3 years.

Figure 1.3: Tree Diagram Goal

To focus on a greatest area of need (GAN), think of the baseline as comparable to the oil checks you would do on your car every thousand miles: You are sampling at the tested grade levels for several years to check the capability of your system. Over time, what has been the level of performance that our third graders (fifth graders, eighth graders, and so on) have reached? This level of performance will vary from year to year, but when you compare multiple years, you will get a good sense of what your school has been able to produce. In the same way, when you sample the oil in your car, you will know how high or low the level is. (It will not tell you why it is high or low; that question comes later.)

Indicators

Indicators are the evidence we look for to see if the goal is being achieved. In the case of school academic goals, indicators are the standards or benchmarks that students have performed most poorly in over a number of years in the GAN (figure 1.4). Using Pareto thinking (focusing only on the "vital few" areas needing improvement for the highest leverage of your time), the selected indicators would be those few standards where performance is the weakest. In our example, in a review of our writing data, we saw that students have been historically weak in "organization" and "mechanics/conventions." We placed these two standards on our SMART goal tree as "indicators." We would want to see strong improvement in these two areas in particular, which will impact improvement in other areas as well.

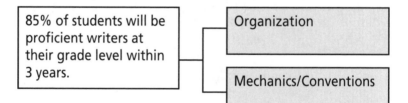

GOAL   **INDICATORS**

85% of students will be proficient writers at their grade level within 3 years.	Organization
	Mechanics/Conventions

Figure 1.4: Tree Diagram Goal and Indicators

Measures

The measures are the assessments you will use to gauge progress on the indicators. In our school example, one measure would be a state/provincial achievement test and another might be a district assessment (figure 1.5, page 21).

Targets

Finally, establishing improvement targets for each measure allows you to track improvement not only by overall average, but also by subgroup (figure 1.6, page 22). Targets can also be defined on a year-by-year basis as incremental steps toward a longer-range

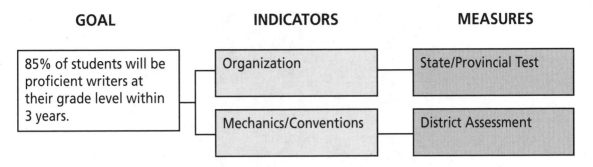

Figure 1.5: Tree Diagram Goal, Indicators, and Measures

goal. In our example, we will set targets for just one indicator and measure. The SMART goal tree shows incremental targets for improving writing organization in years 1, 2, and 3, as well as specific targets for improving writing organization for subgroups with lower baselines by the end of 3 years (special education, English language learners, and minority students).

At a grade or department level, a team of teachers would define "essential learning outcomes"—the specific skills and performances students need to know and be able to do—at their grade level and in a specific subject. At the elementary level, an entire school can easily focus this work on the same vital few areas since all teachers teach all subjects. At the secondary level, teams may find it easier to define essential learning outcomes by individual subjects or courses. In either case, the team would then agree to use—or develop—a common measure to assess student skills and knowledge. An analysis of the results from the common measure would reveal which skills to focus on for improvement. Targets at the classroom level would be established within a shorter time frame and would focus on improving student level of performance from "below" to "at" and "above" proficiency. In our fourth-grade SMART goal tree example (figure 1.7, page 23), the teachers administered a common writing assessment at the beginning of the year, for which they had pre-determined what constituted "above proficient," "proficient," "below proficient," and "way below proficient" performance. From this assessment, the teachers saw that organizing ideas sequentially was one of the vital few

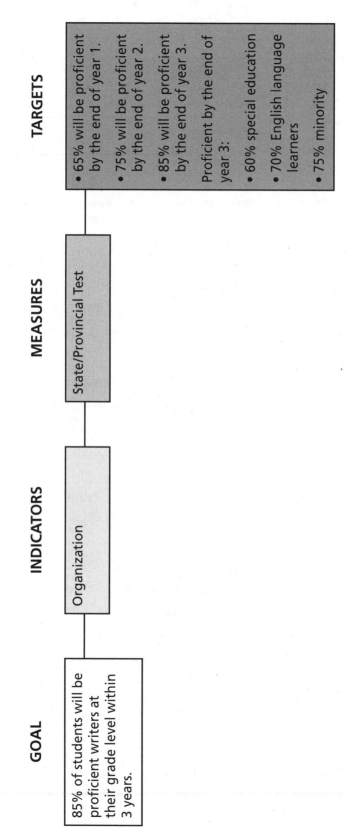

GOAL

85% of students will be proficient writers at their grade level within 3 years.

INDICATORS

Organization

MEASURES

State/Provincial Test

TARGETS

- 65% will be proficient by the end of year 1.
- 75% will be proficient by the end of year 2.
- 85% will be proficient by the end of year 3.

Proficient by the end of year 3:
- 60% special education
- 70% English language learners
- 75% minority

Figure 1.6: Tree Diagram Goal, Indicators, Measures, and Targets

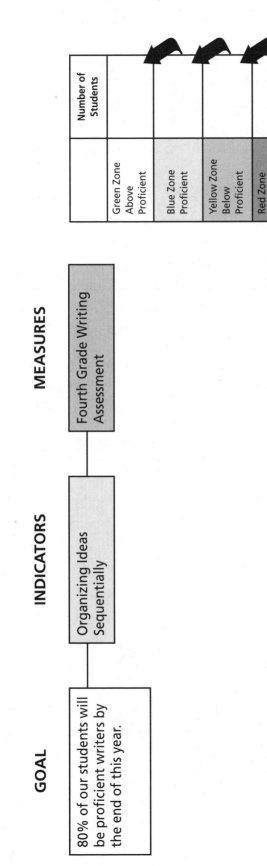

GOAL

INDICATORS

MEASURES

Figure 1.7: Fourth-Grade Team SMART Goal

essential learning outcomes that students did not understand. Next, they will establish specific targets for the number of students they will commit to moving up in proficiency. The highlighting system is a simple visual aid teachers can use in analyzing student results. (For more details on this process, see chapter 4.)

A Process for Implementing SMART Goals

When Schmoker's *Results* book came out, we were impressed by, among other things, his "33-minute meeting agenda." We had been teaching SMART goals and the QLD framework for a few years and were looking for a way to extend SMART goals into a deeper learning process. That was when we developed the "30+ minute meeting process," an adaptation of Schmoker's 33-minute meeting.

The 30+ minute meeting process is a series of five meetings. Each meeting has a specific agenda with time frames and requires that all participants use effective meeting skills, such as:

- Sharing responsibility for facilitating the meetings

- Agreeing to meeting protocols for attendance, participation, and decision-making

- Charting main discussion points and decisions during the meetings

- Recording minutes

- Sticking to time estimates

Work is done between meetings by subgroups and then brought back to the larger group for consideration. The first meeting focuses on establishing the greatest area of need, the second on identifying a SMART goal, the third on correlating promising practices with current practices, the fourth on planning professional development options, and the fifth, after new strategies and professional development have been implemented, on analyzing results and refocusing efforts for further improvement. These meetings can be conducted as a whole staff, by grade-level teams, or by departments. Depending on the SMART goal and its time frame, the meetings can take place over a school year, a semester, or even just a month or two.

The 30+ Minute Meeting Process: Step by Step

Meeting #1: Identify the Need

The purpose of this meeting is to identify *perceptions* of student learning needs. It serves as a way of bringing assumptions to the surface, which builds ownership for examining the actual data.

Between meetings: Verify the need. Between the first and second meeting, a subteam gathers and organizes relevant data, bringing it back to the group in an easily interpreted format for the second meeting. The data needs to show not only the subject area needing the most improvement, but also the skill needs within that subject area. This data will either confirm the group's assumptions from the first meeting or it will raise questions, leading the group to discover a different improvement opportunity.

Meeting #2: Identify SMART Goal

The second meeting is the longest of the five meetings at 65 minutes. The purpose of this meeting is to develop a SMART goal, using the tree diagram, based on a review of the data brought by the subteam.

Between meetings: Conduct a search of promising instructional practices. A subteam is assigned to review promising practices in the goal area, bringing this information back in an organized form to the larger group at the third meeting. The information could be gathered from a review of the literature, observations made in classrooms led by master teachers, workshops or other professional development opportunities, educational research published by universities and other groups, or a combination of these resources.

Meeting #3: Correlate Promising Practices With Current Practices

The purpose of this meeting is to raise awareness about promising practices in the goal area that may not be currently employed by the school. The meeting is also an opportunity to review the group's strengths in the goal area so that those strengths can form the foundation for future work. During this meeting, teachers review the new information brought by the subteam, review their own practices within that context, and determine the new practices they would like to learn in order to have a greater impact on the goal area.

Between meetings: Research professional development options. Between meetings a subteam researches all the ways the teachers might learn more about the promising practices. (See chapter 11 in our book *The Handbook for SMART School Teams*, 2002, to learn about 8 different ways to acquire new knowledge, and the research behind each.) The subteam again organizes this information, bringing it back to the larger group in such a way that individual teachers can select their preferences.

Meeting #4: Plan Professional Development

During this meeting teachers use decision matrices to select *how* they would like to learn the new practices, with choices that may range from engaging in a book study group to observing someone else's classroom to attending a workshop or conference. To build ownership for changing practices in the classroom, it is important that teachers feel as though they are in the driver's seat for determining how they will learn. Some schools have organized this part of the meeting series to require that teachers both sign up for a learning opportunity and volunteer to share their knowledge with others, which is also a powerful learning technique.

Between meetings: Engage in professional learning, implement new practices, and measure student learning improvement. During this phase of the meeting series, a subteam (or several subteams) is responsible for ensuring that teachers get the support they need to learn and practice the new strategies. Using the measures identified in the SMART goal tree, teams of teachers will need time to analyze the impact of their new practices and to make adjustments as they go.

Meeting #5: Analyze Results and Refocus Efforts

This meeting brings the continuous improvement cycle around full circle as teachers review the results of implementing new strategies in the classroom and summarize the lessons they have learned during this process. If the SMART goals have been reached, the conversation focuses on how to sustain the improvements over time—through improved curriculum guides, better assessments, different professional learning options, and so on. The group would then focus on the next greatest area of need, returning to Meeting #1. If results have not been achieved or progress is less than desired, then the conversation will focus on why, and new plans will be put in place.

The 30+ minute meeting series describes the continuous improvement process involved in implementing SMART goals, including data analysis, goal-setting and monitoring, ongoing assessments, testing new practices, and reformulating plans. The process is explained step by step in the feature box on pages 28 and 29. Additional information, including tools and methods for running effective meetings, can be found in *The Handbook for SMART School Teams* (Conzemius & O'Neill, 2002).

Team Reflection: The 30+ Minute Meeting

What knowledge and skills do we need to implement the 30+ minute meeting series?

What information do we need to access?

How does a culture of shared responsibility help support this process?

How does this process reflect best practices in school improvement?

The 30+ Minute Meeting Series

These meetings can be done by the entire staff, by grade level teams, or by departments.

Meeting #1: Identify the need by isolating the opportunity or gap between what is wanted and the current situation.

5 min. Ask the presenting question: What student learning issues are we struggling with the most?

10 min. Brainstorm responses.

5 min. Identify top three priorities by multi-voting.

10 min. Ask: What more do we need to know? How can we find out?

Between meetings, gather student data and information on priority areas.

Meeting #2: Identify SMART Goals for priority area(s).

10 min. Present graphs of student performance in area of concern. (Focus on skill areas or proficiency/ performance levels.)

10 min. Brainstorm results-oriented goal(s) for priority area(s).

5 min. Select one results-oriented goal for each priority area(s).

10 min. Make the results-oriented goal SMART: Individuals write indicators, measures, and targets for one goal.

(Consider indicators by skill/competence/ performance expectations aligned to standards; consider both standardized and classroom- based measures; consider student data when writing targets.)

5 min. Share SMART goals round robin one at a time.

15 min. Have group select "best of" indicators, measures, and targets to write group SMART goal.

10 min. Ask: What do we need to know to affect student learning for this SMART goal?

Between meetings do literature research or best practice review.

Meeting #3: Correlate best practices to current practices.

10 min. Share information gathered between meetings.

10 min. Develop matrix: What are we already doing that supports best practice in this area? What else would we like to learn about?

10 min. Identify instructional strategies we want to do, do more often, or stop doing.

Between meetings, research ways to develop professional knowledge to learn best practices.

Meeting #4: Identify staff development methods we want to use.

10 min. Share information about various staff development methods.

10 min. Use matrix: Individuals select preferred strategy for learning about best practices, identifying areas in which they are willing to coach/teach others.

15 min. Discuss implementation. How will we implement staff development for best practices? What support do we need? How will we measure progress on the SMART goal?

Between meetings, implement staff development and integration of best practices; then gather data to measure against baseline.

Meeting #5: Analyze results and refocus efforts.

10 min. Present graphs of new data.

15 min. Discuss what worked, what did not work, and why.

15 min. If the instructional strategy worked well, discuss how to hold the gains. If the strategy did not work well, decide next steps: START doing the strategy differently, STOP doing the strategy altogether, or START a new strategy.

Start the cycle over again.

SMART Goals Work!

We have taught SMART goals and the 30+ minute meeting process for implementing SMART goals to hundreds of schools: high and low poverty; high and low achievement; rural, suburban, and urban; and schools in the United States and Canada. As these schools have applied the process, they have been delighted to discover how quickly they achieve results. In one case, College Park Elementary—an urban, high-poverty school in Pike Township, Indiana—moved from being one of the lowest performing to one of the highest-performing schools in the district within 2 years. In 2005, Harrison School District, a rural high-poverty district in Michigan, achieved its best results in 8 years, moving off "needs improvement" status for the first time in 3 years.

Even schools that are already very good or great are using SMART goals to become even better. Teachers and students at Adlai Stevenson High School are using SMART goals to continue to improve their performance—even though the school has sustained high performance, earning three U.S. Department of Education Blue Ribbon awards for its achievements. Teachers, students, and parents at suburban Burleigh Elementary School in Brookfield, Wisconsin, have been using SMART goals and formative assessments for the past 5 years and have seen student performance steadily improve from 70% proficiency to 85–90% proficiency across all areas. Teachers in elementary and middle schools in the Muskego-Norway School District in Wisconsin have been using SMART goals for the past 7 years to improve and sustain the performance of their schools. During the last 7 years, one school has incrementally improved third-grade reading achievement from 56% to 94% proficient/advanced, while another school has sustained improvements over the last 2 years to achieve 97% and 99% proficient/advanced—up from 61% in 1998. The entire school district of McFarland, Wisconsin, has used the SMART goals process to focus their efforts in reading. Its schools have consistently raised reading performance above the state average during the last 6 years. The bottom line is this: *The SMART goals process works.*

"I would much rather aim high and fail than aim low and succeed."

—Janelle Juntilla, Music Teacher,
Orono Intermediate School, Orono, MN

As you work to improve student learning, you will need to address curricular decisions, the use of formative and summative assessments, effective ("best" or "promising") practices, professional development, and leadership. This book will provide you with an in-depth look at how each of these factors is made stronger with a focus on SMART goals.

In chapter 2, you will learn how different schools and districts are keeping goals alive through supportive systems, policies, structures, and skill-building. In chapter 3, we link assessment and goals, and we examine the uses of summative and formative assessment in the goal-setting process. Chapter 4 reflects on the power of goals to improve curriculum, instruction, and assessment systems and processes. In chapter 5, we examine professional development practices and take a close look at a school district that believes professional development is at the heart of improvement efforts. Building capacity for goal-oriented thinking throughout a school and district is key to using goals well, and this is explored in chapter 6.

In chapter 7, you will find real stories from elementary, middle, and high schools that are implementing SMART goals and get a firsthand look at their "probletunities"—how they are turning challenges into opportunities for learning and improvement.[1] Chapter 8 wraps up the discussion with a look at renewing our schools, our practices, and ourselves.

---

[1]We first heard the term "probletunity" from Janet Malone, who is with the Poway Unified School District, Poway, California.

There are few teachers and administrators who, when faced with research and concrete examples of what other schools are doing, would not adopt those practices on behalf of helping students. As Mike Schmoker (1999) writes, "Educators are hungry for . . . evidence of exactly how well a method works as well as concrete descriptions of how to make it work" (p. 53). This book will provide you with practical methods and real examples, along with supporting research that will compel you to explore the power of goals in your schools and classrooms. You will gain useful tools, processes, and stories that you can apply in your own schools. When your students begin learning at a faster pace and with greater enthusiasm and you find more joy in work, you will know the effort is worth it.

Chapter 2

Keeping Goals Alive

"So if you cannot understand that there is something in man which responds to the challenge of this mountain and goes out to meet it, that the struggle is the struggle of life itself upward and forever upward, then you won't see why we go."

—George Leigh Mallory
(cited in Hobson, 1999, p. 112)

The process of goal-setting and monitoring is very much one of "beginning with the end in mind," to quote the wisdom of Stephen Covey (1999). The "end" we envision is that by the end of this book you will see goals as a way to fuel, guide, and motivate the work you do each day. It is our hope that framing goals in this way will breathe life into how you lead improvement in your classroom, school, and district. Goals can be a driving force for change; they can be dynamic, resilient, and alive with possibilities. For goals to reach their potential as a high-leverage improvement strategy, we need to keep them in the forefront of our attention at all times. Somehow we need to find ways to keep goals alive on a daily, weekly, monthly, and yearly basis. This chapter explores what that process looks like.

From Survive to Thrive

Let us begin by considering the houseplant as a metaphor. We all know someone who possesses the gift of the proverbial green thumb. And though there is a science and knowledge base of plants called phytology, green-thumbed people everywhere have never studied the science but seem to simply know what to do. These people distinguish themselves from the rest of us by the results they get. You can literally see the difference in the life of their plants.

For most of us, providing regular food, water, and sunlight to keep a plant alive is no big deal. But here is where the distinction becomes evident: For the average person, success is defined as plants that *survive*; for our green thumbs, success is defined as plants that *thrive*. Thriving takes commitment.

Like plants, goals do not have sensory organs that tell them when they need nourishment, nor can they move voluntarily to act on their own behalf. They need attention, care, and knowledgeable people who are committed to their well-being and take an active role in nurturing their growth and potential.

We frequently hear our clients say that they want to make sure their goals and action plans are not put on a shelf and forgotten. They want them to be living, breathing documents. Breathing life into a *document* is no simple matter. In fact, it is impossible. Breathing life into a *goal-setting process* is possible, however, and is exactly what is needed to keep goals not just alive, but also thriving.

Individual Reflection: Goals and Commitment

What goal in your life have you found worthy of commitment? What was the nature of the commitment you made? What are you now achieving as a result of nurturing that goal?

"It is good to have an end to journey toward;
but it is the journey that matters in the end."

—Ursula K. LeGuin
(cited in Hobson, 1999, p. 120)

The Journey: Five Key Questions

In the first chapter we presented a framework—the QLD Framework—for creating strong leadership capacity through focus, reflection, and collaboration. Now we will align a set of powerful questions with that framework to establish a process for collaborative goal-setting and continuous monitoring of goal-related data. These questions are the foundation for the SMART Schools Process, a school-wide curriculum for building professional learning communities. It is this process that provides both the context and the fuel for goals to thrive. Figure 2.1 (page 36) shows the QLD Framework with the five key questions:

- Where do we want to be?

- Where are we now?

- How will we get to where we want to be?

- What are we learning?

- Where should we focus next?

Where Do We Want to Be?

Recall that FOCUS provides direction, guidance, and purpose in the form of vision, values, and a common mission aimed at improving student learning. Also recall that SMART goals help you close the gap between current reality and your vision. The first question in the process, "Where do we want to be?" is a question about *vision*. If there is no vision, or if the vision is only understood or shared by a few, goals will not have a context in which to thrive.

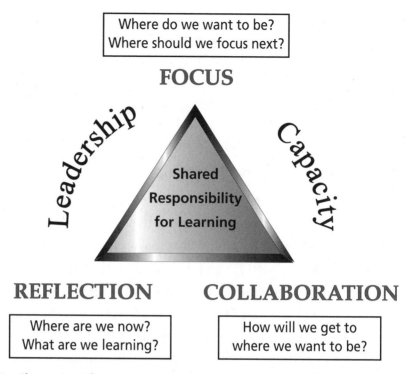

Figure 2.1: The QLD Framework and the Five Key Questions

Second, inspiring visions are built on a set of *values* that the people in the organization identify as essential to their ability to work together. We have found that values are constantly being tested in the goal-setting process. Decisions about what is good enough, what people believe to be possible, what they are willing to fight to protect, and what they are willing to let go of in order to pursue their goals are all value-laden decisions. In cases where the values are being espoused but are not reflected in either the goals or the actions of the people inside the organization, there can be no authentic commitment toward achieving them. Aligning goals and values and then living those values in pursuit of the goals is an essential part of keeping the goals alive.

The third part of FOCUS is *mission,* which describes why we are here in the first place. SMART goals reflect the school's top priority: student learning. When schools engage in discovering, refining, and testing their mission, they sharpen their focus on what really matters. This sharp focus leads them to develop goals to which they can remain committed, thus helping them to stay the course through even the roughest of waters.

Where Are We Now?

We look at our data to answer the REFLECTION question: "Where are we now?" We call this process "reflection" because data, like a mirror, provide us with an objective look at who and where we are. Data help us tell the truth about the results of our work, whether we like what we see or not. By carefully examining our data, we get a picture of how we are doing; however, just knowing how we are doing has limited potential for causing us to change. Knowing how we are doing relative to an inspiring goal is what motivates change. Further, by adding the elements of SMART to our goals, we can be motivated to change in very specific and measurable ways by testing, monitoring, and adjusting specific strategies that will help us achieve our goals more quickly.

How Will We Get to Where We Want to Be?

In the SMART schools process, reflection occurs individually as well as within teams and learning communities. The most powerful way to keep a SMART goal alive is through collective inquiry and collaborative goal-setting using assessments. By adding the element of COLLABORATION focused on formative classroom assessments, we have much better data to help us answer the third question, "How will we get to where we want to be?" Goals that are monitored over time using formative assessments help the professional learning community stay focused on improvement efforts that are having the greatest impact on student learning. Because the goals are collaboratively developed, the community shares responsibility for assuring that they are nurtured and sustained. As Rosenholz (1991) notes, "goal-setting is a purposive, reiterative activity that orients teachers and principals engaged in this process to the school as a collective enterprise" (p. 16).

What Are We Learning, and Where Should We Focus Next?

The process returns us to the REFLECTION corner to answer, "What are we learning?" and then back to the FOCUS corner to answer, "Where should we focus next?" By cycling back to the beginning, the goals are refreshed, revived, and ready to provide guidance and motivation for the next cycle of improvement. When we reflect in the context of SMART goals, we are inspired to modify our actions and activities, to discover new ways of doing things, and to experiment with innovations we might not have tried without the motivation of our goals. Reflection promotes understanding and professional knowledge. When we reflect as a team and share responsibility for goals we have established ourselves, we build a team culture of efficacy and possibility.

Leadership Capacity

In the QLD Framework, leadership capacity, as defined by Lambert (1998), is broad-based, skillful participation in the work of leadership. It is developed as a result of engaging in the five key questions. By examining these questions in an environment of shared responsibility, each person not only learns new leadership skills and knowledge, but also makes important, informed contributions to the development of the organization's vision, mission, values, goals, and ultimately to its success. The process informs and reforms the organization as it unfolds.

"Where do we want to be?" is a foundation-building question, involving all stakeholders in defining the mission, vision, and values of the school. "Where are we now?" is about building what DuFour and Eaker call a "school portrait"—completing a comprehensive and accurate picture of the school's current reality, including the "good, the bad, and the ugly." "How will we get to where we want to be?" answers how priorities are identified, SMART goals are developed, and action plans are implemented to begin closing the gaps between current reality and the vision. "What are we learning?" is a question asked along the way as we implement the strategies and action plans, monitoring our progress and results using ongoing, periodic, and annual assessments on the indicators we have identified for improvement. "Where should we focus next?" is the question asked at the end of one continuous improvement cycle, when gaps have been closed, goals achieved, and lessons documented. This question drives us back to the data to identify the next areas of improvement.

These questions can be applied not only to building a culture of shared responsibility, but even more specifically to:

- School improvement planning

- Program implementation and evaluation

- Classroom action research

- Curriculum development and improvement

- Test analysis

- District strategic planning

They can also be applied to a variety of other situations and can be embedded in a school improvement planning process, as shown in figure 2.2 (p. 40).

Will and Skill

In their seminal report *Successful School Restructuring*, Newmann and Wehlage (1995) synthesized the results of 5 years of research that included more than 1,500 schools across North America and field research in 44 schools in 16 states. The focus of their analysis was to determine which, if any, school restructuring initiatives made a difference in student achievement. They examined a variety of reform initiatives that included structural changes, such as site-based management and teachers working in teams, as well as instructional changes, such as multiyear placements, various grouping strategies, and choice options for parents and students. They found:

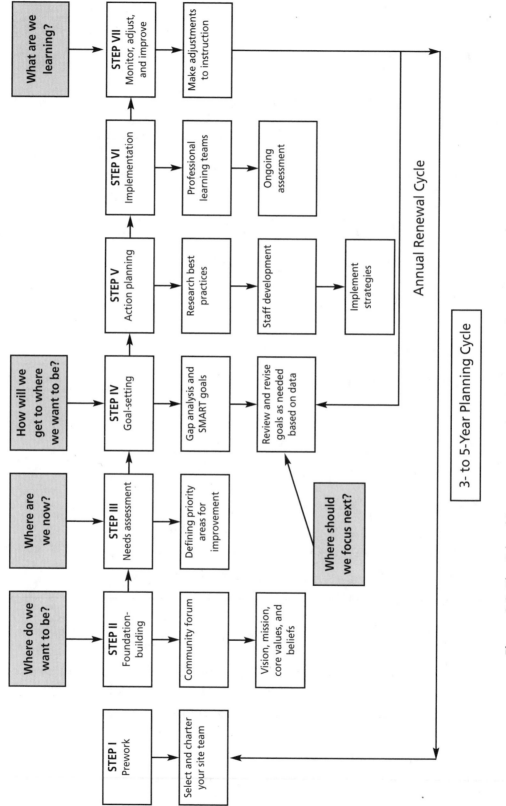

Figure 2.2: The School Improvement Planning Process for Building SMART Schools

"While each of these reforms has some potential to advance student learning, none of them, either alone or in combination, offers a sure remedy. The quality of education for children depends ultimately not on specific techniques, practices or structures, but on more basic human and social resources in a school, especially on the commitment and competence (the will and skill) of educators, and on students' efforts to learn." (p. 1)

It is the compelling nature of a goal that captures and sustains our will to improve. Just as a plant makes its own food by photosynthesis, a goal fuels its own survival through the process by which it was created: collaboration. The collaborative process of developing data-based, results-oriented goals generates and feeds the will to achieve them. As leaders of improvement in schools, teachers and administrators are responsible for breathing life into the goal-setting and goal-monitoring process; they are the caring, nurturing people who provide the sustainable environments in which goals can thrive.

"Technique and ability alone do not get you to the top—it is willpower that is the most important. This willpower you cannot buy with money or be given by others—it rises from your heart."

—Junko Tabei of Japan,
the first woman to climb Mount Everest
(cited in Hobson, 1999, p. 2)

An example of this kind of leadership can be found at Lodi High School, where Principal Laura Love believes that "progress toward our goals provides increasing momentum toward achievement—ours and that of our students." SMART goals developed by teacher learning communities formed around common content and climate concerns provide the driving force for action research occurring throughout the school. These learning communities meet regularly during the school year to monitor their research results and to discuss the impact these results are having on their own and their students' progress. Principal Love negotiates regular "late starts" during the year so that teachers have the time they need to do this work. She also uses staff meetings as a vehicle for checking in on the progress being made. She wrote grants to fund training and supports the work of the teams by embedding their goals in all of their staff development opportunities. She summarizes her school's success by saying, "Of course, the goals must be the teachers', not mine, if they are going to feel true ownership in and power over the outcomes."

What is implied, but perhaps not obvious, in the Lodi example is that in order to keep goals alive, we need to sustain not only the commitment to the goal but also the commitment to continuously improving our skillfulness in pursuing the goal. As Newmann and Wehlage (1995) pointed out, having the will to improve is only part of the equation. We have all experienced a time in our lives when we had a desire to make a change or achieve a goal, such as breaking a bad habit or starting a new hobby. But having the desire did not make the change happen. Why not? In some cases, the desire may not have been strong enough to warrant the hard work needed to achieve our goal. In other cases, we lacked the necessary knowledge or skills to effectively implement the change.

"Excellence is an art won by training and habituation. We do not act rightly because we have virtue or excellence, but we rather have those because we have acted rightly. We are what we repeatedly do. Excellence, then, is not an act, but a habit."

—Aristotle, Greek Philosopher

SMART goals are gap-closing goals: We use them to attain a result that is different from what currently exists. The successive movement toward a SMART goal brings us closer and closer to our desired end state—our vision. Inherent in this definition is the need for change. As Einstein so clearly put it, "Insanity is doing the same thing over and over again while expecting different results." To close gaps, we must change our approach and that most often requires developing new skills.

Team Reflection: Skill Challenges

What are the skill challenges you have experienced as a team? How did you identify and build those skills?

Team Skills: The Three Realms of Skillfulness

Individual Development

There are three realms of skillfulness that need to be considered when thinking about closing gaps. First, the skillfulness needed to execute the change must be considered. It is an important part of moving from mere desire to results. The knowledge and skills needed to implement a change—a particular strategy or a program—can be taught, modeled, learned, and improved. The more authentic and job-embedded the professional development, the faster and more profound the learning can be and the greater the chance that the new skills will be applied and used. Much of these skills can be addressed though targeted, goal-oriented professional development.

Organizational Development

This skill development is complicated by the fact that the use of goals to drive instructional improvement is in itself a change initiative. This second realm of skillfulness affects the way we must support the skill-building. The question becomes, "What is needed for successful implementation and ultimate institutionalization of goal-driven educational change?" This addresses organizational change rather than individual skillfulness. These guiding questions may help:

- Are teachers and administrators skillful collaborators?

- Do they know how to analyze student and system data?

- Can they write measurable goals focused on student learning?

- Are they knowledgeable about the instructional and leadership practices that will have the greatest impact on the achievement of their goals?

- Do they know how to measure or assess the effectiveness of those practices?

- Can they adjust their practices (instructional and administrative) in ways that will better serve their particular population of learners?

Here there is a need to build collective skill in areas traditionally uncharted by educators, and collective skill is needed to fully realize shared responsibility for student learning.

Implementation Management

The third realm of skillfulness is inherent in any substantive improvement: the ability to manage the implementation while continuing to juggle multiple demands within rigid time constraints. It is a little like fixing an airplane while in flight or, perhaps even more appropriately, like continuously redesigning the plane while in flight. This is what educators face every day. And while some find the prospect exhilarating, most find it exasperating.

This domain of skillfulness is often ignored as a part of the overall organizational change strategy, which is why reform efforts so often fail to become institutionalized. In other words, it is why goals die. Without commensurate structural changes designed to support ongoing collaboration and data-driven dialogue, even the strongest-willed, most highly skilled individual will make only so much progress. Individual heroics can take an organization only so far.

Action: Beyond the Plan

Fullan and Stiegelbauer (1991) provide a useful organizational model for thinking about moving from the initial stages of change through implementation and into institutionalization (figure 2.3). The model identifies the key variables needed at each level for keeping the change alive. These variables can be translated into support mechanisms that are needed for keeping goals alive.

Phase I: Initiation	Phase II: Implementation	Phase III: Institutionalization
Change is seen as "high profile."	Change is orchestrated.	Change is embedded in structures and policies.
A clear model is in place.	There is shared control.	Change is linked to instruction.
There is a strong, visible advocate.	There is pressure and support.	Change is in widespread use.
Active initiation exists, including skill-building.	Technical assistance exists.	Competing priorities have been removed.
There is recognition and celebration.	There are rewards.	There is continued assistance.

Figure 2.3: Fullan's Three-Phase Change Model

Fullan's model is a *process*—not a program—for managing complex change with three broad phases: Initiation, Implementation, and Institutionalization. The phases are not necessarily linear; events that occur in later phases can alter decisions made in the early phases, thus modifying the original plan.

Phase I: Initiation

Phase I, initiation, includes the awareness of the need for change as well as the decision to adopt or proceed with the change. For a change to be successful, the change model itself must be clear and understood not only by someone inside the organization who is a strong and visible advocate, but also by those who will be engaged in implementing the change. In order to build momentum, there must be explicit, active skill- and knowledge-building for those who will implement the change, along with recognition and celebration of successes as the change is adopted. According to Fullan, external change agents, working in collaboration with internal leaders, can be most influential at this stage of the change process. When the internal leaders have credibility and clout, and the need is seen as real, visible, and important—in other words, as "high profile"—change is more likely to occur.

Phase II: Implementation

In phase II, the change is implemented through trial and error. Schools that successfully manage change adapt their plans as they go along to "improve the fit between the change and conditions in the school to take advantage of unexpected developments and opportunities" (Fullan, 1991, p. 83). Whether or not the change will be fully adopted depends on the degree of coordination, or "orchestration," provided by change leaders, as well as on the amount of shared responsibility and control the implementers feel they have. It is especially important that implementers not only understand the need for the change at this phase of the process, but that they also see it as very important relative to other needs. Both pressure and support are needed for a change to become fully implemented—pressure in the form of public expectations that the change will be carried out and support in the form of time to adopt the change and technical assistance for the application of new knowledge, skills, and methods. Having a clear vision of what the school should look like when the change is fully implemented is critical, as is some form of reward for beginning to achieve the vision.

Phase III: Institutionalization

Finally, in phase III, the change is solidified through institutionalized practices that are embedded in new policies and structures to ensure that the change is integrated into all aspects of school life. The value of the change to classroom instruction is clear to all, the new practice is in widespread use, and other competing priorities have been removed or at least dramatically reduced. Implementers continue to get assistance for the change, but now assistance is less resource intensive, as implementers begin to modify and adapt the change to meet dynamic student needs. A sign that the change has been fully institutionalized is when it is no longer perceived as an innovation, but instead is simply "the way we do things around here."

Imagine that you want to put a maraschino cherry inside an ice cube. In order to do this, you will need to unfreeze the ice cube. That is phase I in Fullan's model. Next, imagine you put the cherry in the melted water in the ice tray and put the tray back into the freezer. This is phase II. Finally, imagine taking the ice cube out hours later, now frozen around the cherry. Now you have reached phase III.

Success in the McFarland School District

McFarland School District provides one example of a whole system that has been able to institutionalize and sustain improvement over time. In 1998, McFarland, a small suburban district with relatively little racial, ethnic, and socioeconomic diversity, was achieving at or slightly below the state average on state measures of achievement at every level in every subject area. Today, they consistently rank at the highest levels of achievement in reading (96.4% proficiency) at the third grade and have, for 4 years running, outpaced the rest of the state by anywhere from 8 to 12 percentage points in all content areas—despite increasing diversity and significant budget cuts (see figure 2.4, p. 48).

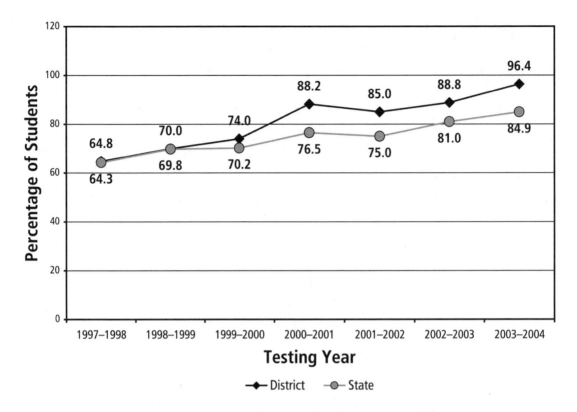

Figure 2.4: McFarland Reading Results; Combined Proficient/Advanced Test Scores

At McFarland, pressure and support play a key role in keeping goals in mind. Pressure comes in the form of public accountability when school teams present their goals and progress to the board of education on an annual basis. Support comes in several ways. The school goals clearly align with the district's strategic goals, which have been a guiding beacon for the district for 5 years. Time, professional development, technical assistance, and removal of other potentially competing priorities have kept the entire system focused on its goals. At the close of every school year, McFarland school leadership teams comprised of teachers, pupil-services personnel, parents, and the principal convene for a 2-day workshop to examine their summative data, to celebrate their successes, and to adjust their goals for the upcoming year.

What McFarland has been able to do so effectively is to build in ongoing support structures and systems that are now simply considered "the way things get done around here." How did they do it? According to Dr. Barbara Hagens, assistant superintendent for curriculum and instruction, "We stayed the course." She and former superintendent Ken Brittingham made a conscious effort to work with the school board, the community, and the teachers to get and stay strategic. Here are the actions they took:

- Kept district priorities and goals unchanged from year to year

- Respected stakeholders' voices and past efforts of school improvement

- Reviewed the current structures, disbanded committees, and created new structures to support district priorities

- Changed the role of the Strategic Planning Committee to reflect a more systemic and visionary approach

- Focused their mission and SMART goals at the school level, closer to what happens in the classroom with students

- Created a calendar for improving student achievement

- Collected data at the building level concerning the four strategic priorities: student achievement, climate, communication, and high expectations

- Provided staff development and training in the four strategic priorities and the SMART goals process

- Required all school goals and plans to align with district priorities by embedding the priorities into school improvement and staff professional development plans

- Chose to pay for curriculum development projects based on the building or school improvement goals and needs

- Redefined the role of team leaders and provided professional development in meeting skills, conflict resolution, time management, and coaching

- Scheduled annual school improvement workshops to examine new data, revise SMART goals, develop new plans, and celebrate success

Goals and improvement are alive and well in this system. One of the key factors is the way in which McFarland moved the responsibility for improvement and goal-setting from the district level to the school level to enhance, not compromise, the focus on district priorities. The district leaders knew that in order to achieve their very lofty district goals, the real work had to be done at the school and classroom levels. Shared responsibility does not come as a response to a mandate; it comes from the active involvement in the development and the pursuit of goals that have meaning for classroom teachers and students.

Team Reflection: Implementing Change

How is change managed in your district, school, and classroom? Do you have a process for managing change? Is it based on a theory of change? What more would you like to know about implementing change?

Nurturing the Cycle of Growth

To return to our original metaphor, for houseplants to thrive, water and sunlight are necessary, but not sufficient. There must also be an environment of caring, support, and patience, along with time for plants to move through their predictable growth cycles. The same is true of goals. As instruments of change, goals must cycle through the predictable process of improvement and must have a supportive, patient, and nurturing environment in which to thrive.

"There are no short cuts to any place worth going."

—Beverly Sill
(cited in Hobson, 1999, p. 61)

If we try to force goal attainment or rush to success, the natural cycle of change will not produce the kinds of results we most desire. For example, too often the expectation is that if we set a goal and make a plan, within a short time the results, as measured by a summative, high-stakes test, will be dramatic. It is a little like planting the seed and then pulling the plant out by the roots once a year to check its progress. Instead, if we patiently provide nutrients (resources) and warmth (support), check progress noninvasively (using multiple measures throughout the year), and then build on small, verifiable successes, we will exceed our initial goals in the long term.

The remainder of this book includes multiple applications and strategies for linking goals to the core delivery systems of education: curriculum, assessment, instruction, professional development, and leadership. In all cases, the environment that surrounds the work will be key to attaining and sustaining the goal. It will be the environment—the culture—that will define the nature and quality of the journey.

Chapter 3

Linking Assessment and Goals

"If we want to create viable alternatives to researchers lobbing information at us, we have to come together in community to engage in difficult forms of discourse out of which shared knowledge is generated."

—Parker Palmer (cited in Sparks, 2003, p. 52)

In a middle school we know, the teachers put in heroic hours trying to help underachieving students learn needed skills and acquire study habits that would lead them to more success. Many of the teachers spend countless hours helping kids after school, reviewing the information taught that day, and cajoling them to put forth more effort and not give up on themselves. Yet in spite of their best efforts, the students who were struggling at the beginning of the year are all too often still struggling at the end.

What is missing? Heroic efforts are not enough—in fact, we may all be working *too* hard as teachers. Were the teachers in this school familiar with the research on feedback, motivation, and goals, they might have engaged students in a powerful continuous-improvement learning process that would have resulted in greater success. This chapter addresses the link between assessment, goals, and shared responsibility for learning. It examines methods for working smarter, not harder.

Team Goals

As Katzenbach and Smith note, "Transforming broad directives into specific and measurable performance goals is the surest first step for a team trying to shape a common purpose meaningful to its members" (1993, p. 53). When teacher teams develop SMART goals collaboratively, they take the first step toward becoming an effective instructional team. The SMART goal tree tool invites conversation about how student learning can best be measured. Creating and administering measures for the SMART goal tree in turn invites ongoing analysis of how students are doing, why some are struggling, and what the team can do to help each other help students learn more.

When teacher teams use the SMART goal tree as part of their ongoing conversations about student learning, they set targets for improvement each time they measure. Achieving (or not achieving) specific targets leads to questions about how to improve instructional practices. When student results are examined collectively, teachers begin asking questions such as, "How are you getting these kids to perform so well?" and "I wonder why I'm not getting these results." When a conversation rises to that level, it becomes truly courageous, because it is then that teachers begin to reveal their own vulnerability and expertise to one another. When teacher teams are tracking SMART goals with specific targets for each measure, they are more focused on why particular skills are weak, and they will then naturally seek to test improvement strategies. The specific goal and targets become the driving force for these conversations. A collective will builds as *we* work to accomplish the goal, pushing each other to go farther *together* than any single one of us could go alone. Not surprisingly, goal-setting and monitoring are self-reinforcing and motivating not only for teachers, but for students as well.

It is not easy to reach this level of courage—especially if we have had negative experiences with data in the past. If we want real and honest conversations, we will need to first establish an environment of trust where it is safe to talk about the good and bad news about student results without fear of reprisal or shame. For this reason, it is very helpful for teams to develop ground rules for using data before they even begin to look at data together. We call these "Data Trust Rules," and they can be quickly brainstormed by a team or by an entire school. Here are some examples of data trust rules from our clients:

- Let the data do the talking.

- We will not use data to blame or shame ourselves or others.

- We're all in this together!

- Keep the focus on the kids!

Team Reflection: Courageous Conversation

What is the "courageous conversation" you're not having as a team? What would it take to have a truly courageous conversation? What would each of you need to have this conversation safely? Generate a list of hopes, fears, and concerns about courageous conversations, and then dialogue to better understand each person's perspective.

Team Activity: Data Trust Rules

Generate data trust rules for your team so that you can work with data, examine your practices, and challenge your thinking together. What can you do to ensure each of you feels safe to stretch beyond your comfort zone?

Assessment That Promotes Learning

Unfortunately, students are often left out of most of our conversations about improving student learning, even though they are the "single most important, irreducible component in the equation of schooling" (Covington, 1992, p. 11). When students get involved in setting goals and monitoring their own progress, their achievement dramatically improves. We now know that when the assessment process involves and engages students in taking charge of their learning, they will try harder and are more committed to learning. In their meta-analysis, Wang, Haertel, and Walberg (1994) first confirmed the value of student involvement in setting and monitoring their learning goals. Later, Black and Wiliam's (1998) study of assessment practices clearly confirmed that *how* students are assessed, and their involvement in that assessment process, has everything to do with whether they are motivated or de-motivated to learn, have confidence to keep trying, or give up. Black and Wiliam's report called for "assessment *for* learning" practices, where students are highly engaged in assessing their learning as an ongoing process. Assessment *for* learning *promotes* learning, addressing the question, "What am I (or we) learning?" Assessment *of* learning, on the other hand, focuses on *evaluating* student results and answers the question, "Have students learned?" Had our middle school team known the power of assessment *for* learning, they would have worked with students to help them set SMART goals and engaged them in effective measurement and feedback practices, helping them focus on what they needed to do to improve and grow.

The Need for Balanced Assessment

Today, with unprecedented pressure for accountability, whether in the United States through the No Child Left Behind legislation, in the Canadian provinces through provincial achievement testing, or in nation-by-nation comparisons such as the TIMMS study, teachers can no longer afford to "teach, test, and hope for the best." With rising numbers of students in special education and an achievement gap that just will not go away, teachers cannot even afford to "teach, test, and try to clean up the rest" anymore. We need to move to a higher level of thinking, where we use a balanced, quality assessment program that serves all users of assessment information, from the boardroom to the classroom, from the policymaker to the student. Accurate summative and formative assessments are needed to inform all users of assessment.

Summative Assessment

Summative assessments are needed to provide information on what students know at a particular point in time. The information from these assessments serves district administrators and policymakers as they make resource decisions at the policy level regarding class size, standards, testing, professional development, and other systemic factors. Summative assessments also serve building-level educators. At the school level, when a school carefully examines its summative assessments, teachers can collectively identify a common greatest area of need, which unifies their efforts toward a single improvement goal. As Emily Calhoun explains, the power of one goal is that "it screens out some of the competing demands for time and attention and affects how resources will be invested" (cited in Sparks, 1999, p. 54). She continues:

> "This focus on one powerful goal limits the amount of student learning data to collect, the amount of data to collect about what is currently happening in curriculum and instruction throughout the school, and the extensiveness of the study of the external knowledge base. It also makes possible the high quality staff development needed to support changes in instruction and the careful study of the implementation of strategies selected by the faculty." (p. 55)

When examined properly, summative assessments can provide important gauges of student mastery of standards, and direct attention to areas that need improvement.

In addition to district administrators, policymakers, and school personnel, the top of the list of assessment users should include the students themselves, followed closely by their teachers and family members, both of whom assist students in their daily learning. With decisions being made in the classroom every few minutes regarding learning and teaching, students and teachers need specific information frequently. Summative assessment, which is occasional and nondescriptive, does not meet the informational needs of students and their teachers.

Formative Assessment

Students need ongoing, descriptive feedback from accurate assessments to allow them to build on their successes and to make adjustments when things are not working. With information from quality formative assessments, students can set SMART goals to meet daily learning targets that move them toward accomplishment of long-term standards.

Teachers need frequent, quality assessment information to guide their instruction. Teachers need to know on a daily basis what is working for each of their students and what is not, and then use that information to support or to change current instructional practices. With quality assessment information on student learning in hand, teachers can set SMART goals aimed at daily learning targets as well as at long-term content standards that students must achieve. When teachers develop assessments that measure student learning targets periodically so that instruction and curriculum can be adjusted, they are using assessment *for* learning. When teachers use these same assessments to evaluate the numbers of students that have mastered the content, they are using assessment *of* learning. When teachers and students use assessment practices to promote more learning, either for the students or for the teachers, they are using formative assessment practices—assessment *for* learning.

Using a balanced assessment program requires courageous conversations at every level of the system. We can't just ask, "Are we doing enough?" We must ask, "Are we doing the right things?" and even more courageously, "Do we know what the 'right' things are?" The use of common measures—curriculum-embedded assessments of student performance that teams of teachers develop, administer, and analyze together—is critical to moving these conversations forward. Ongoing results from these measures provide the platform for the conversation about changing curriculum and instructional practices. When common measures are used both formatively and summatively, they can provide powerful, focused opportunities for improvement. We will next examine how using common assessments in the context of the SMART goals process and engaging both teams of teachers and students will create opportunities for deep reflection and inquiry and lead to improved student learning.

> ### Team Reflection: "Teach, Test, and . . ."
> *Do we "teach, test, and hope for the best" or "teach, test, and clean up the rest"? Is either of these models in effect in our school? What are some questions we could ask to begin moving away from these models?*

Changing Our Practices: Using Common Assessments

Although the solutions to helping all students meet and exceed standards are not always easy to implement, the good news is that they are within our power to discover. If we can stop trying to find the answers "out there" in new programs, curricula, and the latest "quick fix" gurus, and start listening to the expertise already within our schools, we might be surprised by the progress we can make. This is not to dismiss the value of externally investigating promising practices, but it does mean a more careful examination of our own knowledge, skills, and practices to see what we need to do to improve. This requires immense courage and self-discipline. It will mean examining whether *we* truly know and understand what it is that we want students to know and understand. It will mean thinking about assessment differently, as part of the instructional process. And perhaps most challenging of all, it will mean opening our practice to others as we examine student results *together*. This requires us to be vulnerable and to expose our instructional practices to our colleagues, which is not always very comfortable—even when we commit to doing so.

Lori Storer, the former principal of College Park Elementary, a low-income, high-need school outside of Indianapolis, Indiana, kept track of team progress using tools such as team minutes, SMART goal plans, and feedback forms. The teachers at College Park have been deeply engaged in the SMART goals process, involving students in setting their own SMART goals and using SMART goals to talk about student progress during conferences. Storer provided time throughout the year for the teachers to reflect on their students' progress on SMART goals. Here are some of their responses:

Teacher #1: "[My] successes come from (1) frequent communication between the classroom teacher and the English as a second language teacher about academic content and student concerns; (2) a focus on reading skills; and (3) the development of caring relationships through Cougar Clubs [grades 4–5]."

Teacher #2: "Out of 19 students, 17 students improved in reading. However, only 14 out of 19 improved by at least 80%. This equals only 74% of the whole group. As a class the students improved an average of 8 points. This means that some students did exceptionally well while others showed no improvement. The two students who did not improve scored very high on the fall tests. This tells me that when planning for next year, I need to be sure to challenge the high and low students."

Teacher #3: "I feel like my students made more progress in comprehension than my test scores show. My own informal documentation . . . with small groups and individuals and through classroom conversations showed me a much higher level of thinking about reading for both fiction and non-fiction. However, I feel that I didn't adequately prepare my students for transferring that thinking into a standardized test format."

In a culture that values independence and academic freedom, opening our practice truly is a paradigm shift. In the past, we have been accustomed to teaching only "our" students, assessing them in our own way, and looking only at our own students' results. Years ago Emily Calhoun and Carl Glickman (1993) in their work on action research wrote, "Using current data to regularly monitor our students' progress or to examine the implementation of a new curriculum makes great good sense in our pragmatic, information-driven culture, yet for some reason this monitoring remains primarily a private task for each teacher" (p. 14). Susan J. Rosenholz (1991) further notes that the existence of multiple goals at the classroom level "encourages norms of self-reliance and, as a consequence, professional isolation from colleagues" (p. 6). At first glance many teachers might welcome the opportunity for such freedom, but Rosenholz points out the troubling net effect:

> "The absence of professional interaction, or substantive dialogue about their work, carries profound implications: individuals may come to perceive that comparatively few colleagues suffer similar uncertainties about teaching, that they endure fewer instructional problems; and that if others experience few problems, there is embarrassment in admitting one's own." (p. 6)

Many years later, isolation is still a reality in many schools. Committing to using common assessments is the first step out of that isolation, and it is a courageous one.

There is a convergence in the research and literature in acknowledging the power of data at the classroom level. The National Staff Development Council's Professional Standards described in "Innovations Configurations" (2003, p. 49) outline professional development standards that will improve the quality of teaching by providing teachers with research-based instructional strategies and the ability to use various types of classroom assessments appropriately. In *Breaking Ranks II: Strategies for Leading High School Reform* (2004), the National Association of Secondary Principals exhort teachers to "integrate assessment into instruction so that assessment is accomplished using a variety of methods and does not merely measure students, but becomes part of the learning process" (p. 6). In addition, the interest in the work of Rick Stiggins and others has blossomed in recent years, as educators grow in their sophisticated use of testing and assessment to improve student learning.

"The lack of common goals actually promotes isolation from colleagues which animates a spiral of fear and insecurity as teachers perceive that their problems are unique."

—Susan Rosenholz (cited in Schmoker, 1999, p. 25)

"Just in Time" Learning

The phrase "just in time" refers to processes that occur at the moment they are needed. Classroom-based assessment fits into this category. To ensure that each student is meeting or exceeding standards, each school needs to engage in ongoing, shared, formative assessment at the classroom level so that teachers can quickly learn—just in time—what is or is not working instructionally and then make adjustments. Each classroom team will need to focus like a laser beam on those skills that require particular attention and then set SMART goals to prioritize their energy, resources, and time. The measures that teams put in place will be used both formatively (to promote student and teacher learning) and summatively (to assess what has been learned).

Student Involvement in Assessment

In their meta-analysis, Paul Black and Dylan Wiliam (1998) set out to answer the question, "Is there evidence that improving formative assessment raises standards?" The answer was a resounding "yes." They followed with another question: "Is there evidence that there is room for improvement?" And, again, the answer was an emphatic "yes." Attention needs to be given to the use of accurate assessments, descriptive feedback, and student involvement. We need to use the assessment process to build the confidence and responsibility for learning within each student. We need to employ assessment practices that will equip students and teachers with the tools that will inform and promote the learning of all students (assessment *for* learning). These practices, which include setting SMART goals, lead students to demonstrate higher levels of learning gains on summative assessments that audit the student's learning at a particular point in time (assessment *of* learning). Black and Wiliam's research indicates that the achievement gain can be as much as 1.0 standard deviation. More importantly, the achievement gain is greatest for low-achieving students, thus narrowing the achievement gaps within schools.

What might involving students in assessment look like in a classroom? Burleigh Elementary School in Elmbrook, Wisconsin, has fully integrated a balanced assessment system with SMART goals. The school staff annually evaluates summative student results on state tests to identify the greatest area of need by subject and by skills. They establish SMART goals as a school, and then each grade level team develops SMART goals focused on the most important learning standards for their grade level. They have developed common measures, such as writing prompts and running records, which they administer periodically and examine collectively in teams to determine needed instructional and curricular changes. In this process, the teachers have become very clear about the specific learning targets that underlie the standards and have translated these into student-friendly language. The teachers instruct the students using mini-lessons that are very focused on the skills that need improvement. For their part, students continually evaluate their own work, using rubrics and exemplars provided by the teachers. Further, students set their own SMART goals, using the kid-friendly language of the learning targets and focusing specifically on those skills that need the most work based on their own self-assessment and feedback from their peers and teacher. Students review strategies provided to them by their teachers and write "I can . . ." statements as part of a plan that specifies which goals they are working on and which strategies they will use to improve.

If you ask students at Burleigh Elementary what they are working on at any given moment, they will be able to tell you quite specifically. They will also be able to tell you what they need to be working on *next* in order to keep improving. Summative results at Burleigh indicate continuous improvement in all subject areas (proficiency rates are at 90% and above), and the achievement gap for special education and minority students has closed dramatically.

Team Reflection: Engaging Students in Learning and Assessment

To what extent do we authentically engage students in the learning and assessment process? Do we use assessment primarily to evaluate learning or to promote learning, or do we balance these?

The Five Dimensions of Quality Assessments

Rick Stiggins and his colleagues at the Assessment Training Institute of Portland, Oregon, are dedicated to halping educators acquire quality practices that will yield sound and productive classroom assessments. In their book, *Classroom Assessment for Student Learning: Doing It Right—Using It Well* (2004), Stiggins, Arter, Chappuis, and Chappuis identify the following five key dimensions of sound and productive classroom assessments (p. 12).

Dimension 1: Quality assessments arise from and are designed to serve the specific information needs of intended user(s).

Dimension 2: Quality assessments arise from clearly articulated and appropriate achievement targets.

Dimension 3: Quality assessments accurately reflect student achievement.

Dimension 4: Quality assessments yield results that are effectively communicated to their intended users.

Dimension 5: Quality assessments involve students in classroom assessment, record-keeping, and communication of results.

In other words, clear purpose, clear targets, good assessment design, good communication of assessment results, and student involvement in the assessment process underpin sound and productive assessments. Let us look at each of these dimensions integrated with the SMART goals process.

Dimension 1: Quality Assessments Arise From and Are Designed to Serve the Specific Information Needs of Intended Users

This dimension aligns with "clear purpose" in the SMART goals process. When schools implement a balanced assessment program with both quality assessments *of* learning and assessments *for* learning, the informational needs of various users (students, teachers, administrators, and so on) are met. At the policy, district, and school levels, reliable, valid tests that periodically provide clear and accurate information about whether students are mastering standards help educators prioritize resource decisions and set long-term SMART goals for improvement. At the classroom level, frequent formative assessments inform learning and teaching on an ongoing basis, leading to higher levels of achievement as evidenced on periodic summative assessments. Teachers set SMART goals as a team based on dependable information provided by summative testing and common measures that they establish themselves. Students need dependable information to improve their learning, and they rely on clear learning targets in language they can understand to help them set SMART goals. Ongoing, specific feedback on their mastery of these targets helps students adjust their learning processes.

Dimension 2: Quality Assessments Arise From Clearly Articulated and Appropriate Achievement Targets

This dimension aligns with the "specific" element of the SMART goals process. To ensure quality in assessment, the users and developers of assessments must know the specific learning targets that students are to achieve. Learning targets describe very clearly what students must know and be able to do. Standards are the framework in which learning targets reside, but standards tend to be more global, while targets are very specific. In order to engage in high-quality assessment, teachers need to first identify specific learning targets and then to know whether the targets are asking students to demonstrate their knowledge, reasoning skills, performance skills, or ability to create a quality product. The teacher must also understand what it will take for students to become masters of the learning targets: What must students do to acquire knowledge, reasoning skills, performance skills, or the ability to create a quality product? Equally as important, the teacher must share these learning targets and strategies with the students in language that they understand. It is not enough that the teacher knows where students are headed; the students must also know where they are headed, and both the teacher and the students must be moving in the same direction. Teaching and learning about the targets is a journey that students and teachers take together.

When these learning targets are clear to teachers, they can set SMART goals aimed at needed areas of mastery for their students. Once learning targets are clear, students can set corresponding SMART goals in "I can . . ." language based on assessment information the teacher has shared in student-friendly language. See figure 3.1 for an example of a student SMART goal tree.

Dimension 3: Quality Assessments Accurately Reflect Student Achievement

This dimension aligns with the "good assessment design" element of the SMART goals process. Whether teachers are designing assessments to promote or evaluate learning, they should be sure that the assessments will accurately reflect student achievement. Teachers need to use accurate and efficient assessment methods that yield dependable results.

There are four basic types of assessment methods:

- Selected response

- Extended written response

GOAL	INDICATORS

| I can create pieces of writing to tell others what I am thinking or feeling. | I can write sentences with different beginnings. |
| | I can tell that words mean different things. I know when these words add or take away from what I am trying to say in my writing. I know when they make my writing more interesting. |

Figure 3.1: Student SMART Goal Tree in "I Can . . . " Language
(Used with permission from QLD Learning, LLC. The information within the template is used with permission from Leadership, Learning and Assessment, LLC, copyright © 2004, and is based on work from teachers at Cushing Elementary School in Delafield, Wisconsin.)

- Performance assessment
- Personal communication

Selected response methods include multiple choice, true/false, matching, and fill in the blank. Extended written response methods include open-ended questionnaire items and require written descriptions in response. Performance assessments allow students to show what they know through solving problems, performing skills, or creating products. Personal communication occurs when the teacher engages the student in answering questions out loud and then probes the student's thoughts or feelings through a series of questions.

Well-designed selected response and extended written response tests can accurately and efficiently measure knowledge and reasoning targets. Well-designed performance assessments can accurately and efficiently measure reasoning, skill, and product targets. Personal communication assessments can accurately and efficiently measure knowledge, reasoning, and oral skill targets. Each of these assessment types is described in great detail in Rick Stiggins' work. They require that the team have "assessment literacy"—a solid knowledge base on which to make these judgments. The common measure the team develops will be much richer and more reflective of the actual learning targets if the team is knowledgeable about which methods best assess which targets. Figure 3.2 is an example of matching learning targets with assessments.

Learning Target	Type of Assessment			
	Selected Response	Extended Written Response	Performance	Personal Communication
Knowledge	X	X		X
Reasoning	X	X	X	X
Skill			X	X
Product			X	

Figure 3.2: Matching Learning Targets With Assessments

For a student SMART goal, the student would set measures to provide evidence of growth. The SMART goal would also provide information for planning next steps or strategies for moving toward mastery of the standard and underlying learning targets. Figure 3.3 is an example of a student SMART goal tree.

Through SMART goals, the teachers and students set an important direction for improving student learning. It is critical that they have accurate and appropriate assessments to provide needed information for quality instruction and quality learning.

In addition to an appropriate match between the learning target and the type of assessment method, teachers must be sure that they have appropriately sampled their students' knowledge or behavior. They will need to sample enough to reliably know whether a

Linking Assessment and Goals

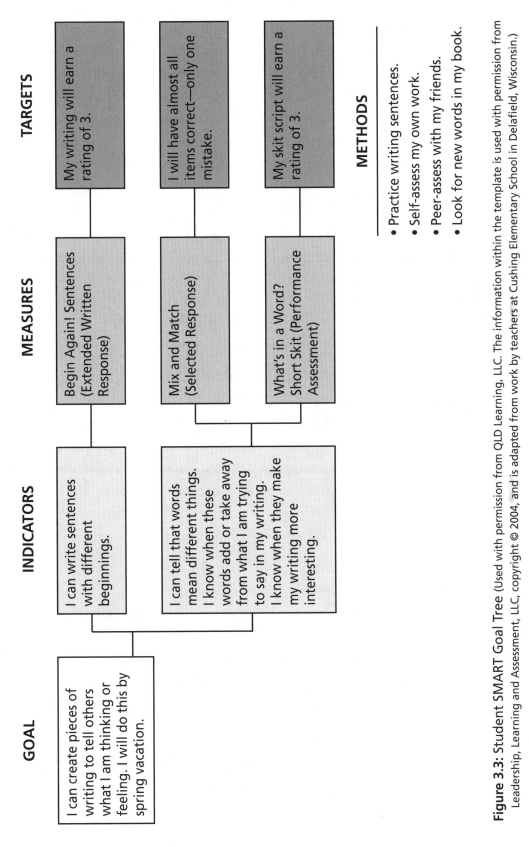

GOAL

INDICATORS

MEASURES

TARGETS

METHODS

I can create pieces of writing to tell others what I am thinking or feeling. I will do this by spring vacation.

I can write sentences with different beginnings.

I can tell that words mean different things. I know when these words add or take away from what I am trying to say in my writing. I know when they make my writing more interesting.

Begin Again! Sentences (Extended Written Response)

Mix and Match (Selected Response)

What's in a Word? Short Skit (Performance Assessment)

My writing will earn a rating of 3.

I will have almost all items correct—only one mistake.

My skit script will earn a rating of 3.

- Practice writing sentences.
- Self-assess my own work.
- Peer-assess with my friends.
- Look for new words in my book.

Figure 3.3: Student SMART Goal Tree (Used with permission from QLD Learning, LLC. The information within the template is used with permission from Leadership, Learning and Assessment, LLC, copyright © 2004, and is adapted from work by teachers at Cushing Elementary School in Delafield, Wisconsin.)

student has mastered the learning targets. Some learning targets, such as those in reading and writing, require extensive measurement over time. The teacher-developed SMART writing goal shown in chapter 1 could be assessed using a common measure formatively to allow for adjustments in teaching and learning before culminating in a summative assessment for accountability. With appropriate sampling, teachers can confidently say that if they were to give one more assessment measuring the learning targets, they could predict how well the student would do.

To avoid the pitfalls of administering an assessment that does not yield the desired information, take a "PDSA" approach—Plan, Do, Study, Act. First, write the assessment and test it on a small scale, preferably on yourselves as a team as well as on several students. Next, make improvements, and then administer the revised assessment.

Finally, teachers must control for bias in assessment. Bias can be found in any assessment method. Bias does not allow the student to show what he or she really knows or can do. The teacher's job is to control for bias as much as humanly possible. Bias can be found in the assessment itself, in the assessor, in the student, or in the environment. Some elements of bias are found across assessment methods, and some are specific to a particular assessment method. Examples of bias include the following:

- Test directions are unclear, such as in a matching item example where students do not know that they can use the same item more than once. (Students might not trust what they know and go instead with a choice that is wrong because the usual practice is not to repeat choices.)

- Test items or questions are unclear, such as a true or false item that is partially true and partially false.

- Evaluators are not properly trained. For example, if all evaluators are not trained to view and understand a rubric in the same way, they will assess student work differently, leading to misjudgment and miscommunication of the actual quality of the student's performance.

- Evaluators are influenced by factors outside of the assessment, such as by previous experience with the student.

- Poor conditions affect the assessment process, such as an assessment being given in a room that is very hot or cold.

- Special circumstances exist for the student being assessed, such as illness or distress during the testing.

- The criteria are vague, such as ambiguity about what constitutes quality work (or a lack of quality).

Teachers and students need accurate, unbiased assessment information to reliably know whether they are meeting or have met their SMART goals.

Dimension 4: Quality Assessments Yield Results That Are Effectively Communicated to Their Intended Users

This dimension aligns with the "good communication of results" element of the SMART goals process. Accurate and dependable information from quality assessments must be communicated to those who need it in a timely and efficient manner. The users of assessment at the policy or instructional support level will need periodic information to help them make sound policy and program decisions. At the classroom level, teachers, students, and their families will need ongoing, descriptive feedback to guide daily teaching, learning, and learning support. As always, both educators and students need accurate information to set appropriate SMART goals for improving student learning.

Clear communication of student learning depends upon a number of factors. First, everyone must understand the meaning of the achievement targets. When larger standards are "unpacked" to uncover the underlying learning targets, they are better understood. For example, if we unpacked the first-grade language arts standard to "produce writing to communicate with different audiences for a variety of purposes," we could identify "Write sentences with varied beginnings" and "Distinguish the uses or meanings of a variety of words (word choice)" as two underpinning learning targets supporting that standard. Second, the assessment information has to be accurate. Educators must be able to rely on the dependability of the information; it should not contain any bias, and it should be proven as reliable over time. Third, an understanding of the symbols used to convey the quality of student learning should be shared among the users of the assessment information. For example, everyone should understand what a "4" means on a test and what it means to be in the 79th percentile. Finally, the assessment information must meet the needs of the intended audience for the information. The information must be at a level of detail and in a language and format that users will understand, and it must be received in a timely manner.

"Valuable achievement can sprout from human society only when it is sufficiently loosened to make possible the free development of an individual's abilities."

—Albert Einstein, Physicist

From a student's perspective, effective communication of progress on learning is critical. When students receive timely, frequent, and descriptive feedback, they begin to see feedback not as a judgment of them, but rather as good information they can use to make important decisions for their own learning. With quality feedback in hand, students can answer three important questions for learning (Stiggins, Arter, Chappuis, & Chappuis, 2004):

- Where am I going?
- Where am I now?
- How can I close the gap?

It is critical for student success that we use quality assessment practices that engage students to know themselves as learners and that help them understand what to do next to improve their learning. Researcher Royce Sadler (1989) states:

> "A key premise is that for students to be able to improve, they must have the capacity to monitor the quality of their own work during actual production. This in turn requires that students:
>
> - Know what high-quality work looks like
>
> - Be able to objectively compare their work to the standard
>
> - Have a store of tactics to make work better based on their observations." (p. 119)

When students have clear, accurate, timely, and descriptive information, they are in the driver's seat for improving their learning. They will work harder because they are clear about what the target looks like and what they need to do to achieve it. They will persevere because they will be proving their own capability by evidence on specific feedback. As a motivational researcher, Martin V. Covington (1992) writes, "In effect, a hard-won success allows students to share the best of two possible worlds: They are seen as *virtuous* by reason of their diligence and as *capable* by the fact of their success" (p. 79).

Individual Reflection: Timely, Accurate Information

Are you receiving the information you need, the way you need it, in time to make decisions about improving your instructional practice?

Who relies on you to provide them with timely, accurate information? Are they receiving what they need, when they need it, in the format in which they need it?

Are students receiving timely, accurate, descriptive information so they can achieve learning targets?

Dimension 5: Quality Assessments Involve Students in Classroom Assessment, Record-Keeping, and Communication of Results

This dimension aligns with the "student involvement" element of the SMART goals process. Underpinning all of the quality assessment dimensions is the critical nature of student involvement. Students can be involved in a wide variety of ways. We can have student-involved assessment, student-involved record-keeping, and student-involved communication of results. Students who are involved in assessment practices can assist the teacher in developing criteria for quality work, evaluate anonymous samples of student work, revise anonymous samples of student work, develop practice items for selected response tests, and give and receive descriptive feedback.

In student-involved record-keeping, students can self-assess their strengths and their need for improvement. They can set SMART goals to improve their learning. This includes identifying their indicators (skills to work on), establishing their improvement targets on key measures, and choosing the strategies they will use to reach their goals and indicators.

Students can also keep portfolios that show, for themselves and to others, what they have learned and where they are headed. Students should select work for inclusion in their portfolios and accompany the work with self-reflections on why they chose the samples and how the samples demonstrate their learning.

Student-involved communication involves students explaining to others who they are as learners. When students articulate their strengths and their areas that need improvement, they state their SMART goals and how they will achieve them. In student-involved conferences, students take the lead in explaining to their parents or guardians who they are as learners. Student-involved conferences are one of the most powerful ways for building student pride and responsibility. When students can show their parents the goals they are working toward and the evidence over time of their attainment of those goals, they feel much more responsible for the learning process and are proud of their ability to lead the way in their learning. As one student said about student-led parent conferences, "It teaches you responsibility. You also learn while you're getting ready. I admit it is hard but you are also satisfied knowing you can prepare a conference like a teacher can" (Stiggins, 2001, p. 493).

Individual Reflection: Conversations

Dr. Bernice McCarthy, creator of the 4MAT System, says that "the attitude of teachers must be to develop the conversations that lead students ultimately back to themselves." What do you think Dr. McCarthy means?

What roles could goal-setting, assessment, and feedback play in this process? What would this look like in your classroom?

What would you change in your individual practice in order to "lead students ultimately back to themselves"?

Involving students throughout the assessment process builds student motivation. Covington (1992) declares that there is compelling evidence that students value ability—sometimes above everything else. Feeling capable contributes to their sense of self-worth. Students feel capable and in control if we involve them in the assessment process, in their own self-assessment and SMART goal-setting, and in the communication of their strengths and areas for improvement. Both their confidence and their learning increase. Covington argues that self-confidence grows through improved performance, and increased confidence triggers further achievement.

If teachers want their students to experience self-esteem, Carol S. Dweck (1999), another motivational researcher, recommends that teachers emphasize learning, challenges, effort, and strategies: "Self-esteem is something students experience when they engage in something fully and use their resources fully, as when they are striving to master something new" (pp. 128–129). Teachers need to help students see that their intelligence increases as they make informed choices on what it will take to succeed. The SMART goals process provides the focus; formative assessment provides the fuel. This creates a powerful learning experience for students and teachers alike.

Creating Winners Through Assessment

With dependable information from accurate formative and summative assessments in hand, students and educators can set goals for improved learning and teaching. Whether educators are setting SMART goals to improve their practice or students are setting SMART goals to improve their learning, the objective is clear: improved teaching and learning practices resulting in student success for all. With a quality, balanced classroom assessment program, everyone is a winner: students, teachers, families, and the community. Each receives the information he or she needs, which results in students who feel confident, possess a greater desire to learn, and gain higher levels of achievement in their learning. Schools win by meeting the necessary levels of accountability.

Of course, assessment is not the whole picture. It must reside in a system of curriculum and instruction management that has mechanisms for continuous renewal and improvement. Curriculum, instruction, and assessment come alive when goals are embedded as part of a continuous learning culture. We will take a look at how this works in the next chapter.

Chapter 4

SMART Goal–Driven Curriculum and Instruction

"Learning is driven by what teachers and students do in the classrooms."

—Black and Wiliam (1998, p. 139)

When Jan was in her first year of teaching, she was confronted with a class of 28 first graders, 8 of whom clearly were already struggling in school. None of these 8 students had mastered beginning level math, reading, or writing skills. Each was "acting out" in his or her own way—one by passively not doing her work and staring out the window, another by throwing crayons across the room when Jan's back was turned, and another by calling out over and over again. Each student was really saying, "I'm feeling like a failure! Help!" Unfortunately, Jan had no tools to help them. She had no curriculum (other than basal readers and math workbooks) and certainly no assessments. She had very little training in teaching reading and early math skills. She worked harder that year than she had ever worked in her life and was sure that very little student learning resulted. Throughout the year, she yearned to talk honestly with colleagues, to tell them she was feeling overwhelmed and did not know what to do, but she was too ashamed. Sadly, by the end of the year, these same students still were not very strong readers, could not do math computations well, and could barely write. At the urging of her colleagues, Jan referred all eight students for special education or Title I services. At the end of the year, she was also crying out for help.

Four years later, Jan was invited to serve as a teacher-leader on the district's K–12 language arts curriculum committee. The language arts curriculum was scheduled for review and change that year, just as math had been reviewed and changed 2 years earlier. Each change cycle required at least 2 years, as each committee clarified objectives, reviewed scope and sequence, and made recommendations for textbooks and other materials. The experience opened Jan's eyes to the larger K–12 perspective, enabling her to see how what she was teaching in the primary grades was clearly linked to the work students were expected to do in later grades. As a result of this experience, Jan became a language arts curriculum leader in the middle school where she later taught. The process of serving on the K–12 committee moved her out of isolation as an independent classroom teacher and into teaming and learning as part of the larger system. As a result, Jan became a stronger teacher and a stronger leader.

Individual Reflection: Curriculum and Transformation

Have you ever had a transformational experience with regard to curriculum? How did you view curriculum when you first entered the profession, and how do you view it now?

Why do we need to focus on curriculum as part of improvement work? For an answer, we need go no further than Bob Marzano's (2003) "what works in schools" research where a "guaranteed and viable curriculum" is the school factor that has the most impact on student achievement. Marzano identifies "opportunity to learn" and "time and viability" as important parts of a guaranteed and viable curriculum. Opportunity to learn refers to whether students have had an opportunity to study a particular topic or solve the particular types of problems tested. Time and viability refer to whether students have had adequate time to understand the topics and problems tested. Marzano further differentiates between *intended*, *implemented*, and *attained* curriculum.

- **Intended curriculum** is content specified by the state, province, district, or school.

- **Implemented curriculum** is content actually delivered by teachers in the classroom.

- **Attained curriculum** is content actually learned by students.

Marzano (2003) claims, "The first school-level factor is a straightforward one: implement a curriculum that is both guaranteed and viable. Yet, enacting this research-based principle of school reform is one of the most significant challenges currently facing U.S. schools" (p. 25). Why is ensuring a guaranteed and viable curriculum such a challenge?

Traditional Curriculum Management

One reason for this challenge is that historically the way we have managed curriculum has been through a "single snapshot" documentation process often led by just a small group of stakeholders. Curriculum improvement usually comes in cycles of 2, 3, or even 5 years. The intended curriculum, often laid out with great specificity in large 3-ring binders, is not very user-friendly to teachers and is therefore not part of their daily lesson planning and unit scheduling. This curriculum becomes an espoused theory, not a theory in action.

Another reason we have had such difficulty implementing a guaranteed and viable curriculum is that we have specified far too many standards and objectives in each discipline, rather than narrowing down to the vital few key objectives students need to master to be successful at the next level. Marzano's group at Mid-continent Research for Education and Learning (McREL) identified 200 standards and 3,093 benchmarks in national- and state-level documents for 14 different subject areas (Kendall & Marzano, 2000). Marzano estimates it would take 15,465 hours to just *adequately* cover these standards, but teachers have only a maximum of 9,042 hours once non-instructional classroom disruptions and interruptions are factored in. Clearly, there is not enough time in the day to cover all this, which is why many teachers simply revert to textbooks and tried-and-true units of instruction with which they are familiar.

A third and perhaps most important reason is that until recently we have not viewed curriculum management through the lens of achievement data. We used to be satisfied once we had documented an aligned scope and sequence—but that was merely the *intended* curriculum plan. When the accountability movement took hold, and districts began viewing student results on achievement tests, the gap between intended, implemented, and attained curriculum was a shock to many districts. This gap became even clearer when, in response to the standards-based movement, states and provinces began using criterion rather than norm-referenced tests. Instead of averages, districts were faced with percentages of students achieving or not achieving the standards of proficiency. Suddenly we were not quite so complacent.

Team Reflection: Your Curriculum

Is there a difference between the intended, implemented, and attained curriculum in your district? What are the causes for those differences?

The challenge now in this age of accountability is how to move from our espoused theory of curriculum to a theory in action. How can we bring the work of curriculum management to life? We believe it is through the goal-setting improvement process.

The Ideal System

Ideally a curriculum in action would be alive and dynamic, continuously improve, and serve the needs of all its primary users—the teachers. It would be based on a rational hierarchy with clear linkages and alignments that describe the essential learning outcomes that need to be mastered for success at the next level. It would show the alignment to state or provincial standards between local objectives, assessments, and units of instruction. It would allow teams of teachers to plan the sequence of units and courses within the instructional time they have with students. It would include valid, reliable, and tested instructional units, strategies, and assessments that any teacher could use in his or her classroom. It would allow for differentiation between learners, addressing the needs of those who need more time or a different learning format as well as those who demonstrate mastery of the content. Most importantly, it would be *owned* by the teachers themselves and used in an active and interactive manner so that it becomes a conversation and a reflective practice, not just a static document.

How do we bring this all together? Through a collaborative, goal-oriented improvement process. As DuFour and Eaker (1998) write, "Without collaborative processes that foster ownership in decisions, schools will not generate the shared commitments and results orientation of a learning community. Thus, the process of curriculum development is at least as important as the final product" (p. 153). For teachers to implement—and want to continuously improve—a guaranteed and viable curriculum, they must engage in a process that helps them "learn themselves through change," as Linda Lambert says. They will need to be in the driver's seat, not just passengers on the bus. They will need opportunities to experience the power of collaboration, reflective practice, and shared leadership. The process will be job-embedded professional development: collegial learning focused at the heart of a teacher's work.

Using Goals to Focus Curriculum Improvement

A goal-oriented curriculum improvement process began in Wisconsin's Madison Metropolitan School District a number of years ago. The district developed a comprehensive curriculum aligned to student learning objectives and state standards, establishing benchmarks at key grade levels. A review of achievement data over time enabled the board to develop results-based goals at the district level to drive improvement in all schools. The district's goals were:

- All students will read at grade level by the end of third grade.

- All students will pass algebra in ninth grade.

- All students will pass geometry in tenth grade.

The board reviewed research that clearly demonstrated how rapidly the brain learns in early years, so resources were focused on the primary grades. They established K–3 assessments in both math and language arts. Reading levels for K–5 were aligned with trade texts, and all elementary schools were stocked with the leveled texts. Writing rubrics and prompts were established to assess the six traits of writing in grades 3–8. Report cards were revamped to reflect the learning standards, and a 4-point scale for each standard was developed (3 is at grade level). Students also receive feedback on their daily assignments based on this 4-point scale.

K–3 teachers are released from their classrooms to conduct the PLAA (Primary Language Arts Assessment) and PMA (Primary Math Assessment) with their individual students, and then results are scored collaboratively. In all the elementary schools, the PLAA and PMA are administered at least twice, once in the fall and once in the spring, and in some schools they are administered three times. Based on the PLAA, students are grouped by ability in leveled texts and put in literacy circles where they focus on different aspects of reading comprehension (summarizing, main idea and detail, drawing conclusions and making inferences, and so on). The six-trait writing process is taught to all students, and regular, formative assessments provide teachers with the feedback they need in order to decide which traits to help students improve.

Madison has become a haven for many families seeking a better environment for their children. The district has an increasing number of students in poverty, many of whom do not speak English as a first language. In spite of these challenges and because of the unrelenting focus on results and ongoing assessment, Madison's schools are closing the achievement gap (Buragas, 2004). Teachers, principals, and board members would be the first to tell you they still have a long way to go, but at least the steps in the journey are very clear and their hard work is beginning to pay off.

Team Reflection: Your Improvement Efforts

How is your district focusing its improvement efforts? Are curriculum, assessment, and instruction all being examined in a particular focus area? What are the payoffs so far?

If your district is not focusing on curricular, instructional, and assessment improvement in a particular area, what has student performance been in the past 3 or more years? What is student performance when you disaggregate the data? Are you seeing steady improvement? If not, it may be time to consider strategically selecting an area for systemic improvement.

The first step in any improvement effort is being able to answer the question, "Where are we going?" The second step is addressing the question, "Where are we now?" Madison provides a good example of a district-led initiative that responds to these two questions. They clearly identified what was important for students to know and be able to do (standards, objectives, and performance proficiencies), as well as how they will measure proficiency (district assessments of reading, math, and writing). The teachers use these assessments diagnostically at the beginning of the year to determine which skills need special emphasis with which students.

As school communities, they use the assessments to focus their school improvement goals on the vital few areas that need improvement. In Madison, teachers use assessments *formatively* to diagnose needs and next steps and to group and regroup students. They use them *summatively* when they administer the district assessments at the end of the year to see how much students have learned and whether their strategies and interventions have been effective.

Madison uses collaborative processes for curriculum work at both the district and school levels. Teachers and administrators use assessment data to focus their work on curriculum, dig deeper into the causes of poor student performance, and to develop SMART goals for improvement. They stay focused in that curricular improvement area, developing formative assessments to better diagnose student needs, researching and testing instructional strategies to see if they help more students learn. In the process, they are deeply engaged in job-embedded professional development, acquiring both instructional and leadership skills as they work in teams. The curriculum is alive, dynamic, and owned by the teachers because they are driving the process.

Curriculum Improvement in Action

Creating a truly robust curriculum in action for all subject areas requires time, discipline, and effort. We recommend starting as Madison did, with an analysis of student results on achievement tests. At a system level, a district should identify a greatest area of need (GAN) and build this focus into strategic priorities. As opposed to a cohort analysis that answers the question of how much growth an individual group of students has made, this review of achievement data is a systems-level study to answer the question, "What has our *system* been capable of producing year after year?" Since math, reading, and writing are so fundamental to success across all subjects, districts would do well to first identify one or two GAN from these three subjects. They should verify these GAN with other measures, examining local assessments as well as national results if at all possible.

In departmentalized schools, if it is clear that writing or reading have been weak, we recommend that the whole school focus on one of these areas for improvement, since both writing and reading have such a strong impact across all curricular areas. If, however, neither writing nor reading prove to be especially weak, then we recommend a departmentalized approach, where each department identifies its own GAN. We discuss this in more detail later in the chapter.

At the building level, schools should evaluate student results for their unique school populations and identify a GAN. By focusing on a common improvement area, they will be able to focus resources and build effective assessments, instructional practices, and strategies across *all* classrooms. By focusing on just one question, Principal Sue Abplanalp and her staff at Lowell Elementary School in the Madison School District discovered that vocabulary was weak across *all* assessments. This realization led them to research and implement effective practices for teaching vocabulary across all disciplines. As a result, the school made remarkable gains in just 3 years (figure 4.1).

	Reading	Science	Social Studies	Math	Language Arts
Baseline	37	37	28	26	19
Year 1	65	73	78	71	59
Year 2	68	85	74	74	64
Year 3	77	73	71	64	61

Figure 4.1: Fourth-Grade Test Scores at Lowell Elementary School

> ### *Team Reflection: Your Goals*
> *Are you focusing on just one goal as a school, or are you pursuing many goals? What goals are your grade level or department teams working on? How are goals aligned or unaligned, and what is the impact on student performance?*

The Team Learning Process

In *Professional Learning Communities at Work*, DuFour and Eaker (1998) outline a process that engages classroom teachers in creating curriculum in action. The process requires that teachers use student performance data at the classroom level to drive instructional and curricular improvements. Called the Team Learning Process, it includes the following steps:

1. Grade- or department-level teams identify the essential learning outcomes for each course or grade level. This answers the question, "What is it that students need to know and be able to do?"

2. Teaching teams develop common, comprehensive assessments to measure the essential learning outcomes. This answers the question, "How will we know if they're learning?"

3. The teams identify proficiency levels all students should achieve on those assessments. This answers the question, "What is good enough? What are our expectations regarding 'quality work'?"

4. The teams review results from the assessments, identify problem areas, and develop plans for addressing those areas. This answers the question, "What will we do for students who are not learning?"

"Unpacking" this process and integrating SMART goals and assessment *for* learning concepts create an improvement strategy that any group of teachers can use to focus their efforts, whether or not there is a school-wide GAN focus.

1. Identify Essential Learning Outcomes

Each teaching team first identifies the essential learning outcomes for their subject area and grade level. Essential learning outcomes are the 8 to 10 "big ideas" per semester-long course or the 16 to 20 big ideas per year-long subject that are most important for students to know and be able to do. As DuFour and Eaker (1998) write, "Because we cannot teach everything in this age of information, a key to establishing a curricular focus is to make sure the curriculum focuses on significant learner outcomes" (p. 163). One difficulty that secondary teachers often complain about is the amount of curriculum they have to cover. The irony, however, is that much of what is being taught in classrooms includes a lot of small facts rather than the important "big ideas." Newmann and Associates (1996) note in their seminal research study that "meaningless school work is a consequence of a number of factors but especially curriculum that emphasizes superficial exposure to hundreds of isolated pieces of information" (p. 23).

One way out of the "coverage" trap is for teams of teachers to step back and identify what is really and truly important for students to know and be able to do, grade by grade and subject by subject. State and provincial curricular frameworks provide vital guidelines, but they are usually either too global or too specific to take the place of this important work. In addition, it is critical that teaching teams feel strong *ownership* of the curriculum—otherwise it is doubtful that there will be follow-through in the classroom.

Let us look in on an eighth-grade math teaching team as an example. They have determined that there are seven essential learning outcomes for the first semester:

- Computation
- Estimation
- Numbers sense
- Measurement

- Geometry/spacial sense

- Probability/statistics

- Patterns, functions, and relations

As they further refine these essential learning outcomes, the teachers will want to consider the *type of learning targets* that underpin each outcome. Learning targets are the specific types of learning that students need to engage in so that they understand concepts. Being clear about learning targets accomplishes two things: It helps teachers clearly communicate to students specific goals for each unit and lesson, and it helps teachers construct high-quality assessments. The Assessment Training Institute describes four distinctly different types of learning targets:

- **Product targets** are those where one must use knowledge, reasoning, and skills to produce a final product. Key words include design, produce, create, develop, and make. In our math team's geometry example, a geometry product target might be to "design a house using only 45- and 90-degree angles."

- **Skill targets** are those where behavioral demonstrations are important, where one must use knowledge and reasoning to perform skillfully. Key words include observe, listen, perform, do, use, question, conduct, and speak. Using our math team example, a skill target might be to "use a protractor to determine the angles of a complex shape."

- **Reasoning targets** involve thinking skills—using one's knowledge to solve a problem, make a decision or plan, and so on. Key words include analyze, compare/contrast, synthesize, classify, infer/deduce, and evaluate. The math team might identify "infer the amount of soil needed for a garden based on given parameters" as an underpinning learning target.

- **Knowledge/understanding targets** are those where some knowledge, facts, or concepts must be learned outright or retrieved via reference materials. Key words include explain, understand, describe, identify, and define. In this case, our math team might generate a list of geometry terms that are important for students to know.

Product	Skill	Reasoning	Knowledge
Design a house using only 45- and 90-degree angles.	Use a protractor to determine the angles of a complex shape.	Infer the amount of soil needed for a garden based on given parameters.	Define geometry terms.

Figure 4.2: Underpinning Learning Targets for Eighth-Grade Geometry

By digging to this depth, teachers move beyond simple declarative or procedural knowledge to a greater refinement of the specific skills and behaviors they would accept as evidence of learning. As Langer, Cotton, and Goff (2003) point out, "It is all too easy to reduce a complex skill into a somewhat 'mindless' area that involves only lower-level learning" (p. 82). We need to guard against oversimplification, pushing the conversation to a "courageous" level: Do we know what the underpinning learning targets are for each learning outcome? Can we clearly articulate them? Have we communicated these learning targets clearly to students? Do we know what to do to teach to these targets?

Our eighth-grade team next translates the learning targets into kid-friendly language so that they can better communicate with students and so that students become more directly involved in their learning. For example, the skill target "Use a protractor to determine angles of a complex shape" becomes "I can use a protractor to identify angles"; the reasoning target "Infer the amount of soil needed for a garden based on given parameters" becomes "I can figure out how much soil will fill a garden space."

2. Develop Common, Comprehensive Assessments

The next step is for the team to think about how they will measure the essential learning outcomes. As described more fully in chapter 3, there are two types of assessments to consider: formative and summative. Formative assessment, according to Black and Wiliam (1998), is "all those activities undertaken by teachers and by their students [that] provide information to be used as feedback to modify the teaching and learning activities in which they are engaged" (p. 140). Providing examples of quality work, using rubrics to evaluate work, and providing students opportunities to self-assess their work are examples of activities that provide feedback that teachers and students can use to modify teaching and learning. Summative assessments, on the other hand, are assessments used to determine how much students have learned as of a particular point in time, and their purpose is accountability. End-of-unit tests, mid-term or final exams, final drafts of writing, and final projects and reports are all examples of summative assessments.

"There are two different kinds of assessments, two different conversations. One is to see how the learner is doing; the other is to find out what has been learned. One is 'On the Way.' The other is 'At the Gate.'"

—Dr. Bernice McCarthy (2000, p. 281)

A common assessment should be used both formatively and summatively. When the assessment is first administered, it is formative—used diagnostically to make pre-instructional decisions. At some point, the assessment should be administered again formatively to assess whether instructional strategies are resulting in students' learning, or whether instruction must be adjusted. "Some point" is determined by the Goldilocks Principle: You need enough information to allow instruction to "take," but you cannot wait too long, or instructional change will be too late to impact learning. In other words, the assessment needs to be at a time that is "just right." DuFour, Eaker, and DuFour recommend at least four times a year to start: "We found that once a quarter doesn't sound too onerous to teachers, so it's a good place to start. Our hope is (and our experience confirms) that teachers will find the process so beneficial that they begin to use common assessments on a more routine basis" (personal communication with Rick DuFour, June 10, 2005).

Of course, common assessments—administered by all teachers on the team at the same time with results collectively analyzed—are not the only time learning is being assessed. There should also be ongoing, student-involved assessment where the students are reflecting on what quality work looks like, reflecting about their own work in relation to quality, and setting SMART goals for improvement. When students are involved in assessment and goal-setting, they can then set SMART goals that are very focused on specific skills and behaviors, and their motivation for learning and improvement grows. (For a more complete discussion of student-involved assessment and goal-setting, see chapter 3.)

The next step in the process is to consider what assessment methods should be used within the common measure. There are four choices:

1. Performance

2. Extended written response

3. Selected response

4. Personal communication

In the case of our eighth-grade team, they have decided which of the learning targets they will assess on their common measure, and they have matched assessment methods to the targets (see figure 4.3, page 92).

Now our team is ready to write their common assessment. One component of a quality assessment is a clear definition of

Learning Targets			
Product Target	**Skill Target**	**Reasoning Target**	**Knowledge Target**
Design a house using only 45- and 90-degree angles.	Use a protractor to determine the angles of a complex shape.	Infer the amount of soil needed for a garden based on given parameters.	Define geometry terms.
Assessment Method			
• Performance	• Performance	• Selected response • Extended written response	• Selected response • Extended written response

Figure 4.3: Matching Learning Targets to Assessment Methods

proficiency: What is good enough? With selected response assessments, the answer may be simply a certain number or percent correct. But with constructed response assessments (performance and extended written response), performance criteria are usually required. Rubrics are essential in this case. According to Arter and McTighe (2001), teachers benefit by using rubrics both in terms of consistency in scoring and improved instruction:

> "The clarity provided by well-defined criteria assists us in reducing subjective judgments when evaluating student work. When a common set of performance criteria and scoring guides are used throughout a department or grade-level team, school, or district, this benefit is extended, increasing the consistency of judgments across teachers." (p. 10)

With regard to improved instruction, Arter and McTigue write, "The vocabulary for describing quality work, and the practice of systematically applying quality criteria to lots of student work, has the potential of turning subjective, informal teacher classroom observation into objective, trusted observations on student progress and status" (p. 12). Although the authors also say this process requires a lot of work at the outset, the long-term benefits in improved instructional practice and improved student learning more than outweigh the time investment. Additionally, we know from the research that when students are involved in applying quality criteria to examining work, they become much more engaged in the learning and improvement process. The clearer we can be as teachers, the clearer we can be with students and the more motivated students will be to learn.

Rubrics come in many forms and scales. (See Arter and McTighe's book [2001] for a veritable treasure trove of rubrics in each subject area and at each level.) The important thing is to collectively agree on what constitutes above-proficient, proficient, and below-proficient performance, and to communicate this clearly to students ahead of time through exemplars for each level. It is particularly helpful to "go visual" at this point—identify scores with colored zones (for example, green is above proficient, blue is at proficient, yellow is below proficient, and red is far below proficient). This way, when it comes time for scoring results, you will be able to create a visual summary of all student scores for all the classrooms and quickly highlight which students fall into which proficiency zone.

As an example, let us return to our eighth-grade team. They have written a common assessment with both selected and constructed response (performance and extended written essay) items. They have developed a rubric for the assessment and aligned it with color-coded zones. The zone chart, which they will use when summarizing results, looks like figure 4.4 (page 94).

Level of Proficiency	Percent Correct	Scale Score (Tied to a Descriptive Rubric)
GREEN— Outstanding! (Above Proficient)	80–100	5–6
BLUE— Very Good! (Proficient)	60–79	4
YELLOW— Needs Work (Below Proficient)	39–59	2–3
RED— Needs a Lot of Work (Way Below Proficient)	Less than 39	1

Figure 4.4: Zone Scoring Chart

In order to avoid the pitfalls of administering an assessment that does not yield the information needed, we recommend taking a PDSA—Plan-Do-Study-Act—approach. Write the assessment, test it on a small scale (preferably on yourselves as a team as well as on several students), make improvements, and finally administer the revised assessment.

3. Identify Proficiency Levels That All Students Should Achieve

To identify proficiency targets, it is helpful to first establish a basis. This is why it is so important to administer the common assessment as early in the year or semester as possible. In addition, teams will need a process for understanding results and determining next steps. We recommend using Bruce Wellman and Laura Lipton's (2004) powerful process for inquiring into data, which they call "The Collaborative Learning Cycle." The cycle is based on a learning process that first invites teams to consider their assumptions, then investigate the data directly, and finally develop solutions. Using this cycle, the team can move scoring from a simple mechanical procedure to a much deeper, more meaningful discussion of student learning.

Wellman and Lipton call the first phase in the cycle "activating and engaging." This phase precedes looking at the data. It is where we reveal our assumptions and expectations about what we think we will see. According to Wellman and Lipton, "Naming and exploring these assumptions before the data is present opens possibilities for reframing and rethinking habits of mind that tacitly and overtly guide instructional decision-making and teaching practices" (p. 45). If the heart of the question truly is "What do we need to change in our instructional practices to ensure each student is learning?" then this step is surely a crucial one.

Imagine our eighth-grade team has administered their common assessment diagnostically as a baseline. Before they score results, the "activating and engaging" questions our team asks include:

- What assumptions do we have about our students?

- What do we expect to see when we look at how our students did on this assessment?

- What questions do we have?

- What are some possibilities for *our l*earning that this experience (of using SMART goals and common assessments) presents to us?

The second phase in the Wellman/Lipton cycle is "exploring and discovering." This is where we analyze the data, the "heart of collaborative inquiry," in Wellman and Lipton's words. It is important in this step that we depersonalize the data, making it emotionally easier to look at. This is not an issue when looking at baseline data from a common assessment, but later on, after instruction has occurred, it would be easy to drop into defensive posturing. The first step begins with the team summarizing their students' scores in one place and highlighting the color-coded zones (figure 4.5, page 96).

Rubric Scores 1–6				
Student #	Class A	Class B	Class C	Class D
1	3	4	2	3
2	6	4	5	1
3	4	2	4	2
4	5	1	3	2
5	1	1	5	3
6	2	3	6	5
7	5	2	1	6

Figure 4.5: Common Measure Summary Worksheet
(Thanks to Rick and Becky DuFour for sharing this format with educators.)

Then, before drawing conclusions about the implications of the results for teaching, curriculum, and so on, our team asks more data discovery–type questions:

- What important points seem to "pop out"?

- What seems to be surprising or unexpected? What challenges our assumptions and expectations?

- What further questions do we have?

This enables the team to look at the data as systematically and unemotionally as possible, before looking into why the results are what they are and what might need to change.

Later on in the process, after the assessment has been administered several times, the team should begin asking about trends and patterns. This will drive their data dialogue deeper as they seek more information about causes and correlations. A moving picture—data over time—always provides more information than a single snapshot.

Once the team has scored results together using the high-lighting zones method, they will see which students are in each color-coded category. This does not answer the question of *why* they are there, but it does give the team a baseline for establishing improvement targets. We recommend that the team discuss how much improvement they are willing to commit to between now and the next time the assessment is administered. How many students can we move from the red to the yellow zone? From the yellow to the blue? From the blue to the green? Putting it all together in a tree diagram, the team now has a result to aim for with a focus on important skill areas, a common assessment, and specific improvement targets (see figure 4.6, page 98).

Team Reflection: Reviewing Results

Do we review the results of our students' assessments together as a team? Do we have a method for analyzing these results? How might the methods discussed here improve our effectiveness in examining student work?

4. Review Results, Identify Problem Areas, and Develop Plans for Addressing Those Areas

The third phase in Wellman and Lipton's Collaborative Learning Cycle is "organizing and integrating." In this phase of the model, we generate theories, do some problem-solving, and begin looking for possible solutions. When we separate problems from solutions, we are clearer about causes, and our solutions can be more targeted. At this point, our eighth-grade team asks:

- What conclusions can we draw from looking at our students' performance?

- What explanations can we think of for their performance?

- How might we verify our explanations? What other data sources can we think of (such as interviews with the students themselves and with other teachers, literature reviews, and so on)?

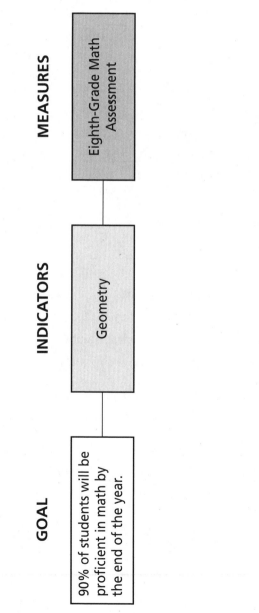
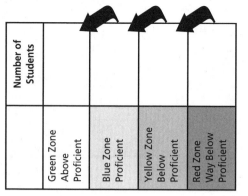

GOAL

90% of students will be proficient in math by the end of the year.

INDICATORS

Geometry

MEASURES

Eighth-Grade Math Assessment

	Number of Students
Green Zone Above Proficient	
Blue Zone Proficient	
Yellow Zone Below Proficient	
Red Zone Way Below Proficient	

Figure 4.6: Eighth-Grade Math Team SMART Goal Tree

Before we turn to solution-finding, it is important that we stay open to multiple voices and multiple perspectives so that we do not end up with solutions that are merely satisfying: minimally addressing the problem or gap. Why not jump to an obvious solution? As Mike Schmoker (1999) points out, "The history of education is littered with attempts to ensure that teachers have learned to use certain innovations. What is less certain is the depth of that learning, whether learning was even remotely connected to student growth" (p. 29). When teachers collectively investigate research on effective practices, they are much more invested in the application of that research. An added benefit is that in conducting this research—reading selected articles, books, and videos, speaking to knowledgeable experts, and dialoguing about what they are discovering—teachers begin to question their assumptions about good teaching in ways they had not done before.

Strong evidence for this is found in Sue Abplanalp's study of her own school, Lowell Elementary, mentioned previously in this chapter. When teachers were fully engaged in a self-discovery process of goal-setting, research, dialogue, self-selected professional development, instructional implementation, and ongoing assessment, their teaching practices improved and student results improved. Abplanalp measured the degree of implementation of best literacy practices in teachers' classrooms using Fullan's 3-stage change model. She added "inquiry" to capture knowledge-building as a phase. At the start of the change process, only 12 teachers had institutionalized these practices in their classrooms; by the end of the year, 21 (out of 30) had done so, and the rest were implementing the practices (see figure 4.7, page 100).

Some excellent sources for research on effective practices include Marzano's "What Works" series, *The Handbook on Effective Instructional Strategies* by Myles Friedman and Steven Fisher, and Fred Newmann's groundbreaking research on "authentic achievement." Newmann's work deserves special mention here, as

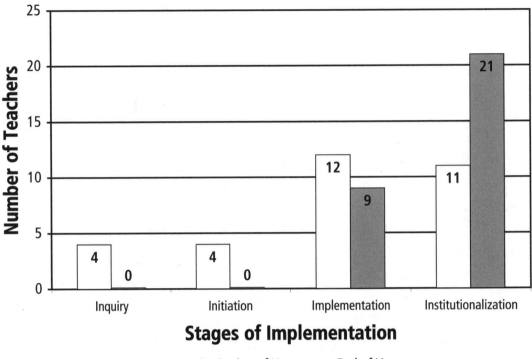

Figure 4.7: Lowell School Implementation of Literacy Practices: Beginning/End of Year Comparison of 30 Teachers

he and his colleagues led one of the most rigorous, comprehensive analyses of student performance ever conducted. Newmann and Associates (1996) writes:

> "The term *authentic achievement* . . . stands for intellectual accomplishments that are worthwhile, significant, and meaningful, such as those undertaken by successful adults. . . . For students, we define authentic achievement through three criteria critical to significant intellectual accomplishment: construction of knowledge, disciplined inquiry, and the value of achievement beyond school." (pp. 23–24)

In response to critics who would argue that authentic pedagogy neglects teaching basic skills and important content, thus preventing students from performing well on high-stakes tests such as college admissions, the authors found that "students in the [research study] schools demonstrating the highest levels of authentic pedagogy performed as well as or better than other comparable students in terms of standardized test scores" (p. 43).

The implications of Newmann's work are profound: Teachers need to understand how to provide intellectually high-quality and engaging work and assessments for *all* students if students are to achieve at higher levels. This will require understanding what intellectually high-quality, challenging work and assessment look like. Newmann describes these in great detail with supporting rubrics.

> ### Team Reflection: Effective Instructional Practices
> *What are some effective practices that we have read about recently, and how do these relate to our instructional improvement goals? How could we learn more about effective instructional practices?*

Our eighth-grade team will want to look at which students fall into each zone and do a careful analysis of those students' learning needs. Then they will investigate instructional strategies using literature reviews, books, publications, videos, internal experts, and other sources, bringing these strategies back for discussion as a team and committing themselves to trying them in their classrooms.

Principals can support teams in this important work by providing structures and templates for planning and improvement. When teams are expected to plan together, and the principal provides an organizational system for tracking and following up on plans, improvement work becomes part of "what we do" as a school. When those structures and templates emphasize standards, goals, assessments, instructional strategies, and professional development, they reinforce what is important for teachers to focus on. Most importantly, when principals use these documents to follow up by providing encouragement and removing barriers, curriculum, instruction, and assessment improvement becomes a living, breathing process. Figures 4.8, 4.9, and 4.10 (pages 103–107) are samples of templates principals are using to reinforce these concepts.

"I would rather fail than not have a chance to fail. . . . You learn from failing, and I have learned not to be too hard on myself, not to get down on myself. . . . It has made me a better player."

—Chris Snelling, Seattle Mariners Left Fielder

Putting It All Together

The purpose of all curriculum improvement should be to improve student learning. We know from the research that for students to learn well, they must be full participants in their learning process (Black and Wiliam, 1998; Marzano, 2003; Newmann & Associates, 1996). In order for students to be fully engaged in the learning process, teachers must be clear about the curriculum and improvement process, and schools must be structured to support the work of teachers who are supporting the students. What might this look like if we put it all together, through the eyes of the student, the teacher, and the school? One of our clients in Lewiston, Idaho, has done just that (see figure 4.11, pages 110–111). The three perspectives—student, teacher, and school—are held in place with three core questions:

- Where am I going?

- Where am I now?

- How can I close the gap?

Where Am I Going?

For students to be able to answer "Where am I going?" they need to fully understand learning targets. For this to happen, teachers must provide a clear vision of the targets in student-friendly

(continued on page 108)

Team/Department Goal-Setting Form

Team Members: _____

The team will have a weekly conversation regarding goal progress. We will meet on

_____.

Building Goal #1:

Building Goal #2:

1. Write one team goal based on one of the building goals. It should answer the question: "What do we expect them to learn?"

2. List the strategies that the team will use to achieve this goal.

   Strategy:

   Strategy:

   Strategy:

(continued)

Figure 4.8: Team/Department Goal-Setting Form

3. What will be the indicators of attainment? (This should answer the question, "How will we know what they have learned?")

4. What resources are needed to support this goal?

5. How will we respond if a student does not learn the material?

6. What will we do for students who have already mastered the concepts or skills?

Courtesy of Elmbrook School District
Tonawanda Elementary School, Brookfield, Wisconsin

Figure 4.8: Team/Department Goal-Setting Form (continued)

Pre-Observation Report

Teacher Name: _____

Curricular Area:_____ **Date of Observation:** _____

Time of Observation: Start _____ **End** _____

LESSON PLAN SUMMARY

1. What is the objective of this lesson? <u>What do you want the students to learn?</u>
   (This is different than what you want the students to do.)

2. What outcome(s) from your curriculum guide does this lesson support? (Look at
   your curriculum guide.)

3. What specific content, topic, and/or skill will be taught? (Please indicate if this is
   a new, practice, review, or diagnostic lesson.)

4. What teaching strategies will you use to accomplish this objective? (For example,
   these include modeling, lecture, small group, individual, and so on.)

(continued)

Figure 4.9: Pre-Observation Report

5. What will you expect the students to do? (If applicable, please attach copies of any handouts students will use.)

6. How will you assess their learning? <u>How will you know if they learned it?</u>

7. What opportunities will be included for differentiation of instruction?

8. What will you do if students do not learn it?

9. Does this lesson reflect any of the building goals and/or your professional goals?

10. Are there any special circumstances or specific students you want the evaluator to be aware of and/or observe?

11. Does this lesson build on recommendations from a previous evaluation this year?

Courtesy of Elmbrook School District
Tonawanda Elementary School, Brookfield, Wisconsin

Figure 4.9: Pre-Observation Report (continued)

Post-Observation Report

This report should be completed by the teacher prior to the post-conference and brought to the meeting with the principal.

Teacher Name: _____

Date and Time of Post-Conference: _____

Please reflect on the lesson taught and answer the following questions:

1. What instructional skills did you use in the lesson that you feel were effective in promoting student learning?

2. As you think about your lesson and the learning that occurred, what changes would you make?

3. Please provide an update of your team goal or professional goal for this year.

Courtesy of Elmbrook School District
Tonawanda Elementary School, Brookfield, Wisconsin

Figure 4.10: Post-Observation Report

(continued from page 102)

language. For teachers to be able to do this, the school or district must have articulated the most important student learning outcomes and aligned these outcomes with standards.

Students also need to know what "good" looks like from having seen examples of good performances or responses. Teachers must use examples and models of strong and weak work to help students discern what is good. Schools must have a shared understanding of the evidence of good work they will accept for the learning targets.

Where Am I Now?

Students need to know where they are so they can improve. To do this, they must understand their strengths and weaknesses with regard to the learning targets. Teachers must support students by offering frequent, descriptive feedback and modeling reflective practice themselves. They must provide students with opportunities to self-assess and set new goals based on that assessment. Schools need to provide time for teachers to collaboratively score student work.

Students need to know how to articulate where they are so that they can improve. They should know how to use criteria for selecting work to include in their portfolios and how to lead conferences with their parents in which they explain why the work was selected. For students to do this well, teachers need to be able to explain the purpose of portfolios and how to select work samples. Schools need to provide the criteria and protocols for student-led conferences to ensure continuity and a focus on student learning.

How Can I Close the Gap?

Students need to understand the tasks they are being asked to engage in and understand how the different parts of the task add up to the whole. The task must have meaning for them. For this to occur, teachers must design lessons that focus on one aspect of quality at a time and teachers must be able to explain how all the components of the lesson add up to a greater whole. They will need to design instruction so that it fully engages the students' brains, helping them see connections and patterns. The school in turn needs to support teachers by creating processes that will ensure a guaranteed, viable curriculum. Achievement data must be regularly reviewed to assess student progress on the standards and to inform instructional improvements.

Students need to review and revise their work for quality and better understanding. Teachers in turn should support students by providing ongoing opportunities for revision after feedback and exemplars for revision. Schools need to provide rubrics for scoring and professional learning time to deepen each teacher's understanding of formative assessment.

Students need to be able to track, reflect on, and communicate progress. This requires that teachers provide instruction that encourages reflection through written and oral means as well as deeper, more reflective questions. Schools should facilitate professional learning time that deepens each teacher's understanding of higher-order thinking skills. They must also establish year-long calendars of the scope and sequence of curriculum to ensure equitable opportunities to learn.

Finally, students need to see connections across all the disciplines. Teachers can support this by using research-based strategies (such as Marzano's [2003] nine best practices or Newmann's [1996] standards for authentic pedagogy) that transfer across all content areas. Schools should provide opportunities for teachers to learn research-based strategies and to dialogue about the implications for improving their practice.

A Living, Breathing Process

Richard Elmore (2000) writes that "instructional improvements occur most frequently as a consequence of purely voluntary acts among consenting adults" (p. 7). He goes on to say,

For the student to answer . . .	The student must . . .	That requires the teacher to . . .	We support this as a school or department when we . . .
Where am I going?	Understand and articulate learning targets	Provide clear and understandable vision of learning targets	Know and state clearly what we want students to learn
	Know what a good performance or response looks like for the learning target	Use examples and models of strong and weak work	Have a clear and common understanding of acceptable evidence for the learning targets (How will we know they have learned?)
Where am I now?	Understand strengths and weaknesses with regard to the learning target	Offer regular descriptive feedback that is criterion based, timely, and corrective in nature	Facilitate collaborative scoring of student work
	Self-assess and set new goals	Model and teach reflective process	
	Using an established criteria, select a work sample for portfolio that proves a level of proficiency and explains why the piece qualifies	Define portfolio components and common assessments	Provide criteria and format for student-led conferences focused on student learning
How can I close the gap?	Understand task(s) they are being asked to engage in and how the component parts add up to the whole	Design lessons that focus on one aspect of quality at a time	Ensure alignment between written, taught, and tested curriculum
		Teach each component of a task and ensure students understand all the parts and how they ultimately come together	Analyze student achievement data and use the information to inform instruction

(continued)

Figure 4.11: Goal-Setting for Improved Student Achievement

(Designed by Ellen Perconti and Bob Donaldson, Independent School District # 1, Lewiston, Idaho. Based on PLC, Assessment for Learning, and the SMART goals process. Used with permission.)

For the student to answer . . .	The student must . . .	That requires the teacher to . . .	We support this as a school or department when we . . .
How can I close the gap?	Review and revise work for quality and understanding	Provide opportunities to revise following feedback Provide exemplars for students to revise and respond to regarding how to improve	Provide extra time—study table Develop bank of exemplars and anchor papers Develop common scoring rubrics Promote professional learning regarding formative assessment
	Track, reflect on, and communicate progress	Provide instruction on and opportunity to reflect on performances or work. This might include: • Writing a process paper detailing how they solved a problem • Writing about a piece of work, explaining where they are now and what they will do next • Reflecting on growth • Engaging in higher-order questioning strategies	Mentor students Facilitate professional learning regarding thinking- and problem-solving strategies Engage in higher-order questioning practices Establish instructional calendar and curriculum mapping to ensure equitable instruction
	See connections of learning across disciplines	Use research-based instructional strategies that are not subject-specific but transfer between content areas	Provide opportunities for learning research-based strategies, encourage dialogue about implementation, and support action research

Figure 4.11: Goal-Setting for Improved Student Achievement (continued)
(Designed by Ellen Perconti and Bob Donaldson, Independent School District # 1, Lewiston, Idaho. Based on PLC, Assessment for Learning, and the SMART goals process. Used with permission.)

"Schools are . . . almost always aboil with some kind of 'change,' but they are only rarely involved in any deliberate process of improvement, where progress is measured against a clearly specified instructional goal." When teams of teachers collaboratively develop SMART goals in the context of curriculum work, barriers of isolation break down, and the kinds of questions they ask change:

- What is important for our students to know and be able to do?

- What evidence will we accept that they know it?

- What are the instructional strategies that are most effective with students?"

"Curriculum" should be a living process that engages all learners—students and teachers alike—in being clear about focus, having the means for reflecting on what is being learned, and experimenting with strategies for improvement. SMART goals provide the focus, context, and process for curriculum, instruction, and assessment improvement work. When teams of teachers come together around a common goal for improvement, using a data-driven, standards-based curriculum-improvement process, their learning deepens, their practice improves, and student learning increases. Throughout this chapter, there has been an unwritten assumption: Teachers have the knowledge they need in order to use good assessment practices and improvement strategies. However, this knowledge is not addressed in most teacher preservice programs, so schools must make a concerted effort to build in strong professional development. In the next chapter, we will examine the power of goals to drive professional development decisions in order to accelerate staff learning.

Chapter 5

Using SMART Goals to Drive Professional Development

"For it is the ultimate wisdom of the mountains that man is never so much a man as when he is striving for what is beyond his grasp and that there is no battle worth winning save that against his own ignorance and fear."

—James Ramsey Ullman
(cited in Hobson, 1999, p. 142)

When Anne began her career in education, she was excited, nervous, confident, and scared—a mix of emotions that was both intense and exhilarating. She had an opportunity to make a difference in the lives of children, as well as an enormous responsibility. With great enthusiasm, she accepted a position as a school psychologist in a small rural school district. She soon discovered that her new job required her to perform duties for which her university training had not prepared her. She remembers her heart pounding as she wondered, "What's this thing called 'in-service,' and why am I in charge of it? What does a gifted-and-talented coordinator do? How do I supervise the migrant programs? How can I be the junior varsity girls' basketball coach?" She realized that she needed a plan, and she needed it right away.

Fortunately, she had been assigned a mentor: Dr. Juanita Pawlisch, also new to the district, was its first-ever director of special education. Pawlisch was to be Anne's supervisor as well as her coach. Anne recognized from the moment she met Pawlisch that there was something very special about her: She was an avid learner. She was focused, goal-oriented, knowledgeable, and constantly seeking opportunities to learn. She was a living, breathing example of SMART goals in action; she was on a life-long journey of self and organizational improvement.

Collaboratively, the two of them set out to create Anne's individual professional development plan. It began with an examination of the district's goals for meeting the needs of all children, followed by Anne's self-assessment of her professional learning needs. The data from this assessment ultimately led to a set of individual professional goals for both Anne and Pawlisch. Next, they developed a specific plan for how to achieve those goals. The professional development plan for Anne included:

- Reading the research
- Working with teachers to bridge new learning with its classroom application
- Dialoguing with other psychologists in the county about emerging state and federal laws that guide special education programs and processes
- Honing her observational skills as a way to broaden her assessment repertoire
- Learning new psychometric tools

Pawlisch's plan included her own development goals along with strategies for helping Anne achieve hers.

This plan was very helpful, but what about those other duties Anne had been assigned? For example, she was to be chair of the in-service committee. How was *this* plan going to help her with *that* responsibility? The answer was clear: The process she just went through at a personal level was the same process that would help her lead this district team toward a data-driven plan for organizational learning. But first she would need to know two things: (1) the district's strategic priorities and goals and (2) the staff's assessment of their needs relative to the district's vision. But the old way of doing things took over as Anne set out to discover this crucial information.

To assess staff needs, Anne's committee drafted a checklist of all the current topics they could find in their review of brochures and program materials. Each staff member checked the topics he or she was interested in learning more about. What the committee received, of course, was a disconnected array of topics representing a wide variety of "wants" rather than a focused set of learning needs; however, the committee was accustomed to providing a menu of disparate but mandatory in-service activities, so members began making arrangements for various workshops and programs based on the levels of interest shared on the checklists.

This was the point at which Anne noticed a significant departure between what she was living and what she was leading, and it began to cause her considerable discomfort. In her conversations with Pawlisch, Anne was focused on standards and goals, job-embedded results, and data-driven decision-making. She was *living* what is known as the National Staff Development Council's (NSDC) Standards for Professional Development (Hirsch, 2001). What she was *leading* was the 1970s version of what Kelleher (2003) calls "adult pull-out programs": "These activities, which may or may not be connected to a particular school or district goal and often have no follow-up, tend to amount to a series of disjointed experiences that do not necessarily have any observable effect on education" (Kelleher, 2003, p. 751). Anne's own professional goals and plan included a series of periodic evaluations, opportunities for reflection, updates, and adjustments. The district's in-service "plan" and offerings did not even include the most basic level of feedback on satisfaction with the content, delivery, and location of the offering.

Individual Reflection: Your First Day

Think back to your first day on the job. What were your apprehensions? What were your needs? Did you have specific goals and a plan for achieving them? What would have helped you the most?

Linking Goals and Professional Development

It is with guarded optimism that we say the days of professional development as a laundry list of the latest fads or some group's or individual's personal interests are gone. As consultants, we still get last-minute calls to fill a staff development day that someone scheduled but forgot to resource. In those cases, we politely decline the opportunity unless we are able to detect a strategic direction or broader set of goals that our work could legitimately support. Simply stated, there should be a link between goals and professional development.

This chapter is organized around three types of goals in which professional development is a key element:

1. **Organizational Goals**—district, division, school, grade-level, or departmental goals

2. **Individual Professional Goals**—staff and administration goals

3. **Student Learning Goals**—classroom, subgroup, or individual student goals

Although all three types (or domains) of goals ultimately lead toward improved student learning, the focus of professional development methods, content, and evaluation strategies may change based on which type is driving professional development choices. It is critical to align the three domains so that the greatest collective impact from professional development can be realized.

Organizational Goals

Organizational goals help us focus and filter our learning on the system's highest priorities. In this way, professional development and organizational improvement are integrally related. The growth of professionals can contribute to the organization as a whole, but individual growth without the organizational context is insufficient and inefficient in helping the organization achieve its strategic goals. In the absence of organizational direction (vision and goals), the impact of professional development becomes a matter of luck rather than the result of a deliberate allocation of resources.

When we view this relationship from the opposite perspective, we see an equally strong case for linking the two. Imagine a district or school strategy for improvement that ignores the need to develop the people who will be responsible for implementing the improvements. It is hard to divorce the two, to imagine one without the other—especially in an educational environment where the organization is almost synonymous with its people.

The Kimberly Area School District in Kimberly, Wisconsin, provides a dramatic example of how a district-wide vision, accompanied by a clear set of SMART goals, not only shaped professional development practices, but ultimately redefined the role of professional development as *the* key strategic process for improving student results. In Kimberly, every decision is based on the pursuit of goals; everything they do to achieve their goals is considered professional development.

In the mid-1990s, the board, central administration, and principals published a strategic plan for the district that they called Mission Possible: Raise Student Achievement. The plan included a goal that by the 2002–2003 school year at least 90% of students would be proficient or advanced readers as assessed by the Wisconsin Reading Comprehension Test (WRCT). The leaders believed strongly that if children could read and read well, the scores on other measures of achievement in other areas of learning would also dramatically improve.

At the time that the plan was created, the average proficiency rate for young readers in Kimberly was at 61% on the WRCT (below the state average) and between 40% and 50% on the Wisconsin Knowledge and Concepts Exams (WKCE). The district's goal of 90% seemed unattainable and unrealistic to those deep inside the organization. In fact, there were accusations that it would hurt kids; many felt that becoming so narrowly focused on reading meant that the social, emotional, artistic, physical, and broader knowledge-based needs of students would be ignored. Furthermore, it was feared that such dramatic gains could only be accomplished if teachers did nothing but teach to the test.

Indeed, this goal would be impossible if the district had not supported a fundamental change in how teachers taught and how students learned. In particular, the plan for achieving this lofty goal needed to include a change in how professional development was delivered, how classrooms were resourced, what content was taught, and ultimately, what was removed from the already over-filled plates of the staff.

The graph in figure 5.1 illustrates Kimberly's 7-year journey. Based on the reading performance of third graders as measured by the WCRT, Mission Possible was indeed possible. Kimberly was the only district to improve its rank on all three subtests in every year at every grade level tested. As a result, based on a formula that included a variety of criteria, Kimberly ranked first among all Wisconsin districts as the most improving school district. It moved from the bottom half of the districts in 1998–1999 to the top 20% in the state in 2003–2004.

Recall that one of the fears of staff was that if the district were to take such a narrow approach in targeting resources and staff development on literacy, other areas of learning would be compromised. However, the district's leadership believed that by focusing on reading, other areas would benefit. It turns out the district was right.

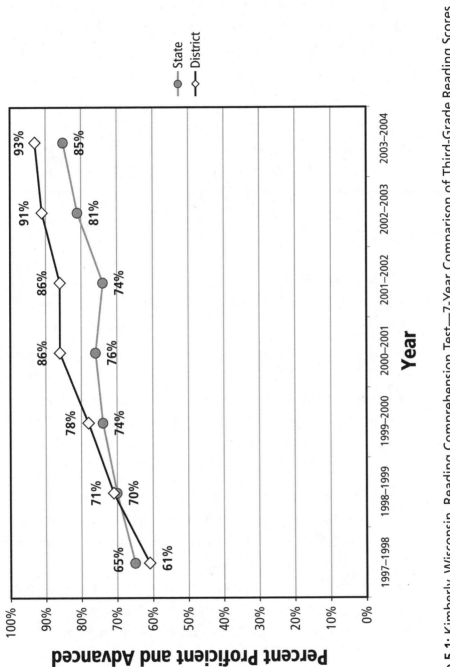

Figure 5.1: Kimberly, Wisconsin, Reading Comprehension Test—7-Year Comparison of Third-Grade Reading Scores. Percent proficient and advanced.

Proving the power of the Pareto Principle, student performance in *all* subjects improved at all tested grade levels (figure 5.2). Kimberly's results as measured by the Wisconsin Knowledge and Concepts Exam (WKCE) started at or below the state average and moved to well above the state average leading the district to be recognized by the Wisconsin Taxpayers Alliance as "a high-achieving, low-spending" district.

When asked how they did this, the answer was swift and certain. According to Mary Bowen-Eggebraaten, the district's assistant superintendent for learning, "The entire system became a learning organization focused on classroom implementation of instructional best practices." Essentially, she meant that everything was at stake.

How They Did It

Kimberly began by focusing its efforts in the area of early literacy, targeting all elementary staff development and program resources to the implementation of best practices in reading assessment and instruction. In collaboration with Viterbo University, Kimberly's leadership team designed and delivered a graduate program focused on classroom implementation of best practices in teaching for learning. The courses were taught by principals, central office administrators, and eventually by teacher-leaders.

The development model at the elementary level includes ongoing collegial learning teams in which teachers regularly work and learn together, sharing their strategies and examining their data. One of the formal graduate courses embedded in this model begins in August with a 2-day intensive training session on designing and implementing standards-based lessons. The outcome of this session is a lesson that is implemented within the first week of school. Following the implementation, a teacher has time to reflect on student learning from the lesson and share insights with the administrative supervisor, a person who has been trained as a standards-based learning coach. A new standards-based lesson is then developed and implemented while a trained coach

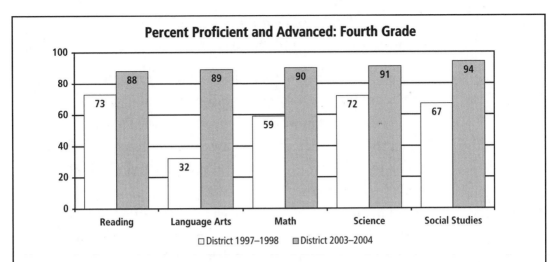

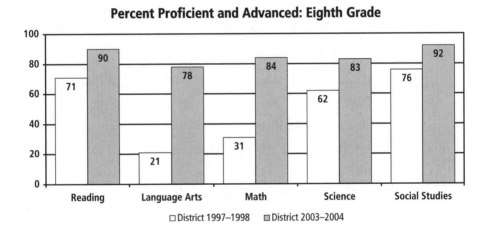

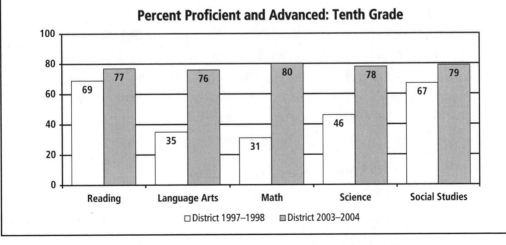

Figure 5.2: Kimberly, Wisconsin, WKCE 7-Year Comparisons for Fourth, Eighth, and Tenth Grades.

observes. The two reflect together and discuss teacher learning and improvements. This cycle is repeated throughout the year.

Another approach creates a learning laboratory where children participate in a summer session designed to give teachers a safe environment in which to receive valuable feedback on implementation strategies. In these sessions, the teacher-student ratio is two to one—two teachers for every one child. One teacher teaches while another teacher observes. Then, in a fashion similar to Japanese lesson study (Lewis & Tsuchida, 1998; Watanabe, 2002), they come together to dialogue about what worked, what did not work, and what could be done differently to achieve maximum results. Then the teachers rotate roles so that both have the opportunity to teach, to observe, and to give and receive descriptive feedback.

At the middle school, every teacher participates as a member of a "tuning protocol" team, "a [professional development] process through which educators can hone their skills by examining student work in a supportive, problem-solving group" (Easton, 2002, p. 28). In Kimberly, the process was designed by and is still led by teacher-leaders. It is cross-disciplinary, happens during the day, and is grounded in research-based best practices in assessment *for* learning.

Team Reflection: A Strong Focus on Student Learning

Staff development focused directly on student work and/or involving peer observations and feedback can be a high-stakes endeavor. How does being a member of a supportive team with goals focused on student learning help to make these kinds of professional development opportunities less threatening?

The Importance of Leadership

In a system, it is not enough to change the behaviors of one part of the organization—in this case, the teachers. It is the very nature of systems that all of the individuals and their respective roles are symbiotic and, as such, must realign in support of the change effort. Thus, Kimberly also needed to change how leadership occurred so that there were systematic and informed support mechanisms in place for teachers to successfully implement what they were learning. "It's all about leadership," says Bowen-Eggebraaten. "Leadership is no longer a 'position' assigned to a certain group of individuals; it is the responsibility of everyone in the organization. All individuals are expected to take responsibility for improving student learning results. When a system is accountable for results, it translates into shared leadership."

Obviously, this definition of leadership challenges the traditional role of both principals and teachers. To move toward this kind of leadership model, principals need to learn to become effective coaches, and teachers need to learn the skills of leadership, including how to use data to inform and guide their instruction. In Kimberly, teachers in the early grades regularly assess and monitor student reading levels using a variety of assessment tools and techniques. At the beginning of the year, they know which children are struggling with specific aspects of reading, and they adjust their instruction accordingly. They meet with their grade-level colleagues to analyze results and discuss new strategies.

Principals now look for evidence of student learning as their primary coaching and decision-making vehicle. Teachers report the reading levels of all students on a monthly basis so that principals can make resource adjustments as needed. Reading resource teachers are assigned based on student performance needs and are reassigned periodically throughout the year based on data. This continual adjustment of resources and strategies based on student need and results is just one example of how Kimberly has used its strategic goals and student performance data to drive decisions.

"Only those who risk going too far can possibly
find out how far they can go."

—T. S. Eliot (cited in Hobson, 1999, p. 64)

It all started with what most considered an unattainable goal. But the goal was only the beginning of the journey for Kimberly. The goal alone would not have led to the results they are experiencing today. What the goal did for them was to focus their energy and resources. Linking the goal to targeted, results-oriented, job-embedded staff development that made the real difference in student performance.

Individual Reflection: New Learning
When in your life has a goal motivated you to learn something new?

Individual Professional Goals

Do organizational goals supersede individual goals? We are frequently asked this question for which there is no single definitive answer. What is sometimes implied in this question is an "us versus them" culture, which is a sign of nonalignment to the mission rather than of confusion over the relationship between goal levels. A better question, perhaps, is "How can organizational and individual goals work in harmony to the benefit of all—especially to the benefit of all of our students?" Individual professional goals are a critical component of a full system of accountability and responsibility, not a subtext for the organizational goals. There are several reasons why individual professional goals are necessary, and why, if properly focused, they will automatically align organizationally.

Goals for Beginning Teachers

First, just as the story at the start of this chapter illustrates, the individual professional goals of a novice educator are not, nor should they be, the same as those of experienced educators. The literature on professional development for new teachers suggests that they struggle with things that are second nature and therefore basically invisible to the experienced teacher (Freiberg, 2002; Moir & Baron, 2002). Because their needs are different, the processes and methods for their professional development may also be different.

"Few new teachers begin their careers fully understanding the complexity of helping students meet their potential. Most struggle with curriculum issues, classroom management, and the varied demands of districts, administrators, parents and colleagues."

—Ellen Moir and Wendy Baron (2002, p. 54)

According to Moir and Baron (2002), "a crucial part of beginning teachers' professional development is formative assessment, the process of systematically identifying areas for growth, setting personal performance goals and developing the skills needed to attain these goals" (p. 54). The authors identify three basic elements of an effective formative assessment and goal-setting system for new educators: standards, criteria, and evidence:

1. Standards provide the "what" that skill and knowledge gaps can be assessed against.

2. Criteria define how much improvement can be expected so that new teachers learn that "regardless of their initial abilities, they can systematically move to higher levels of practice."

3. Evidence helps teachers analyze the "how" of their practice, a key skill that is especially important to new teachers.

The examination of evidence encourages a more reflective practice in which teachers use data to plan, design lessons, assess instructional impact, and adjust their teaching methods. With all three of these elements in place, "as new teachers assess their own work and strive to meet their goals, they gain confidence that despite the many challenges they face, through targeted professional development they can become excellent teachers" (Moir & Baron, 2002, p. 55).

Goals for Experienced Educators

For experienced educators, the challenges are more likely to be related to changing one's practice. This is not because what teachers have been doing is wrong or ineffective, but because of the changing environment in which they find themselves. For example, the data may show that an instructional practice that has worked fine for years is no longer achieving the same result. It could be that a previously homogeneous student population has now become very diverse. Challenges presented by the infusion of new technologies, new information about the brain and learning, new assessment techniques, new mandates that require a different set of skills, or new research that reveals the power of collaboration will all require the experienced educator to learn new skills. For experienced educators, focused goals are more important than ever before so that they are not overwhelmed by the number of changes they are being asked to make. How does one eat the elephant? One bite at a time.

Team Reflection: Learning Needs

How do the learning needs of relatively new and experienced teachers on your team differ? How can each of you support the others, regardless of your years of experience?

Goals That Are Motivating

Individual professional goals are also powerful sources of motivation. When teachers set professional learning goals based on self-identified professional growth challenges, the goals are more compelling. When teachers can relate their goals to better outcomes for the children whose faces they see every day, the goals are more meaningful. And finally, when teachers develop individual professional goals that take them incrementally to a personal career vision, the likelihood of remaining committed to the goal over the long term is enhanced. In this way, professional development designed to achieve these motivating goals becomes an exciting opportunity as opposed to an imposed mandate.

Goals Focused on Student Success

When organizational goals and individual professional goals are focused on student success, they will align. Our experience tells us that the alignment problem comes not in the individual or organizational intent to achieve better learning outcomes for children, but in how the goals are typically stated. So, an appropriate response to the "us versus them" question might be to take a deeper look at the organizational goals. We might find that they are not student success goals at all, but rather mandates in disguise. For example, professional development that is sponsored by the district or school division and aligned to a goal that states "All teachers will use the XYZ Writing Process" is a mandate, not a student success goal.

Is it okay for the district to require a consistent process be used to teach writing? Yes—In fact, it is probably a good thing. However, in the world of SMART goals, it is the ultimate result that defines the goal, not the processes used to get there. When defining the goal as an end result, teachers will have the opportunity to employ many techniques and strategies, including the district-determined programs, to get the job done. Thus, a goal that states "All students will demonstrate proficiency in writing" speaks to every teacher's desire to help students be successful writers. In planning for professional development, the goal, stated in this way, allows individual teachers to self-assess their specific professional development needs, which may or may not begin with learning how to use the XYZ Writing Process. Finally, this goal allows for use of a multitude of professional development methods that are much more standards-based, job-embedded, and results-oriented than a workshop on the XYZ Writing Process.

"Staff development that improves the learning of all students organizes adults into learning communities whose goals are aligned with those of the school and district."

—National Staff Development Council (2001, p. 11)

Individual professional goals ought to lead to improvements in instructional practice and therefore can be stated in terms of the educator's own learning goals versus student learning outcomes.

Let's look at an example of a SMART teacher goal focused on improving the teaching of reading (figure 5.3). The goal, "Increase the use of strategies and resources for teaching reading comprehension," is a teacher learning goal. Research has established that a teacher's knowledge and use of instructional strategies and resources are directly linked to student achievement (Marzano, 2003). When a teacher demonstrates growth in this area and documents implementation of these strategies through classroom observations, lesson plans, and reflection, student achievement will be enhanced. As Candace McKay (2004), a master trainer for Charlotte Danielson's work, notes:

> "The very process that teachers go through to reflect on their practice, self-assess, determine areas of strength and weakness, and to relate those areas to student learning goals is a teacher learning experience in itself."

The process McKay describes is a highly effective, job-embedded professional development practice. Additionally, the goal tree helps to focus and define potential professional development needs. For example, differentiating instruction is an indicator of increased use of strategies and resources for teaching reading comprehension. If this teacher has not had the opportunity to learn how to differentiate instruction based on specific student learning styles, skills, and needs, the professional development need for the teacher becomes obvious.

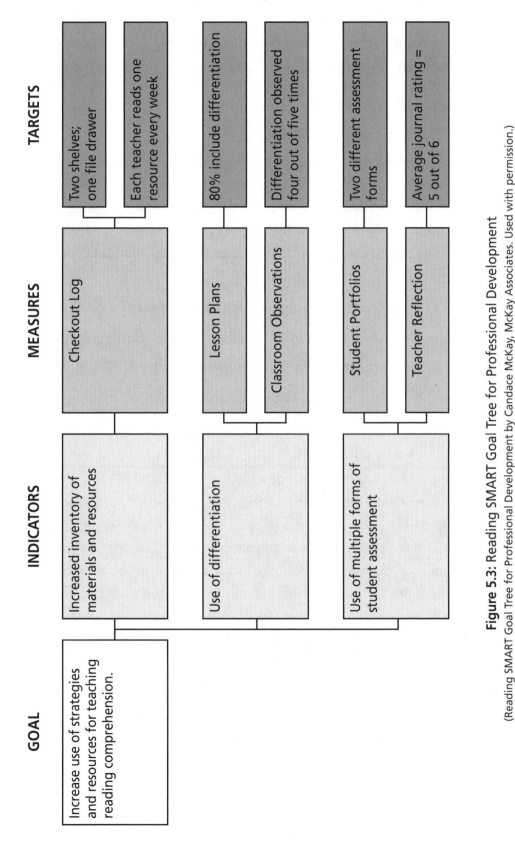

Figure 5.3: Reading SMART Goal Tree for Professional Development

(Reading SMART Goal Tree for Professional Development by Candace McKay, McKay Associates. Used with permission.)

Individual Reflection: Focus on Learning
Create an individual learning goal tree based on some aspect of professional growth you would like to pursue.

Student Learning Goals

The closer you get to the child, the more specific your goals should be and the more frequent your monitoring of those goals should be. Goals based on authentic, formative assessments, diagnostic analyses of individual student needs, or both give the greatest guidance to curricular and instructional decision-making. Consider the following examples:

- Differentiated instruction based on measurable skill gaps

- Instructional design based on student learning styles

- Content enrichment or remediation based on standards

- Content remediation based on assessment of specific knowledge

Once a skill or knowledge gap has been identified for a child or a group of children, the decision about how to close the gap becomes the critical responsibility of the teacher. Preferably, this would happen as a team of grade-level or department teachers come together to share strategies, brainstorm, learn new practices, and test new practices that are focused on a very specific set of student needs. The strategies would be implemented. Because the diagnostic tools and assessments are in place and the results are being monitored on a regular basis, teachers could then quickly see whether their new learning was having the desired impact. They could then adjust their teaching—or not—based on the data. What could be more job-embedded and data-driven when it comes to professional development?

Here is another way to think about the link between student learning goals and teacher professional development: Let's say that the student learning goal is to improve the problem-solving skills of freshman algebra students by 20% overall. Using a variety of ongoing assessments, observations, and applications, the teacher determines that there is a group of students in each of her four sections of algebra who consistently demonstrate a weakness in creating algebraic formulae in real-life applications. Several questions need to be asked:

- First, have these students been taught how to apply algebra concepts in real life? Is this part of our curriculum now or previously?

- If yes, then ask, is there some reason these students missed this part of the curriculum—are they new to the school, or chronically absent or truant? Is it part of our regular instructional practice? If not, why not?

- Does the teacher know how to teach application-based algebra?

Through a step-by-step process of analyzing student learning needs and developing a SMART goal focused on a specific skill, a teacher might detect her own professional development needs and thus be able to target her own learning directly toward improving the performance of her students on that very specific skill. This is an action-research approach to both professional development and instructional change.

> *"Action research is continual professional development—
> a direct route to improving teaching and learning."*
>
> —Emily Calhoun (2002, p. 18)

At Morton East High School in Cicero, Illinois, Ann Banaszak is using a student learning goal tree as a means to engage her high school chemistry students in individual goal-setting to support their learning. Her classroom SMART goal (see the goal tree in figure 5.4) gives everyone in the class a clear picture of what she expects

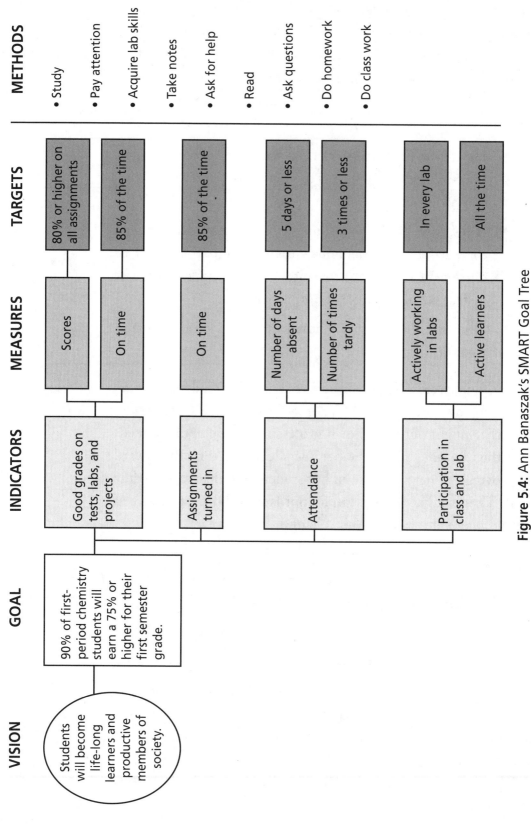

Figure 5.4: Ann Banaszak's SMART Goal Tree

while delineating the specific criteria that define achievement of that goal (indicators). They also know how success is going to be measured, the amount of improvement that is considered desirable, and finally, the strategies that she and her students can use to achieve the goal. How does knowing this help Banaszak develop as a professional? As she monitors the progress of her class against these indicators and targets, she will discover areas where changing her practice might move the class farther, faster, deeper, or more fully toward the goal. That is how meaningful professional development can be derived from a student learning perspective.

It does not matter whether the student learning need is skill- or knowledge-based, in a core academic subject or an elective, or whether the state tests a particular skill or knowledge. Setting and using student-focused goals linked to content and performance standards can lead to highly focused professional development that results in better learning for students. When a goal is student-focused, the desired outcome reflects a situation that is different from the current state. Doing more of the same is not likely to result in dramatic improvement. Thus, there is an implied need to change. Professional development becomes the teacher's vehicle for making research-based changes in his or her practice.

Team Reflection: A Profound Change

Discuss a professional development scenario you have experienced that profoundly changed your approach either with an individual child or with an entire classroom or subject.

Evaluation of Professional Development

All goals should lead to successful student learning; this is obvious. What is not so obvious is how professional development can consistently be designed, delivered, and evaluated toward this end. How can we know whether our goals are better achieved because of the professional development practices in which we have engaged? For this we turn to the excellent work of Thomas Guskey (2002, 2003). He and his colleagues provide a five-level model for professional development evaluation. The model is cumulative in nature; it moves to progressively more rigorous criteria, with each level building on the success of the previous level.

- **Level 1:** Participant Reactions
- **Level 2:** Participant Learning
- **Level 3:** Organization Support and Change
- **Level 4:** Participant Use of New Knowledge and Skills
- **Level 5:** Student Learning Outcomes

A brief explanation of each level will help to illustrate its progressive nature.

Level 1: Participant Reactions

This is probably the most commonly used evaluation process. It measures satisfaction with the experience and is typically performed at the end of a professional development event such as a workshop or meeting. Various elements of the experience are explored via a survey or questionnaire or even through verbal self-reporting. Participants might be asked to comment on or rate how valuable the event was, how relevant or useful the material was, how well the material/ideas were presented, how satisfied they were with the overall experience, or a combination of these questions.

Level 2: Participant Learning

This level of evaluation focuses on what participants felt they gained in terms of new knowledge or skills, how they anticipate applying or using their new learning, or both. This level could even include an assessment of the new knowledge or skills, whereby participants are asked to demonstrate the new learning in some way. Self-reflections and portfolios are also Level 2 strategies. Portfolios might include samples of student work that reflect the teacher's new approach, journal entries made by the teacher that document reflections on his or her new learning, a new lesson plan or activity that was created as a result of the new learning, and documentation of interviews with parents, students, or fellow teachers that are related to new learning.

Level 3: Organization Support and Change

There is a simple mathematical principle that can illustrate the power of Level 3 evaluation. Using a multiplication formula, one can predict the success of any professional development activity that takes place in an organization. Here is how it works:

> If satisfaction = 10, learning = 10, and organizational support = 10, then the formula for success is $10 \times 10 \times 10 = 1000$.

Guskey notes that at Level 3, "you need to focus on questions about the organization characteristics and attributes necessary for success" (2002, p. 47). In other words, do policies, resources, reward structures, and the organization's mission and goals align with and support the implementation of newly learned strategies? If not, then change at the organizational level must occur before the investment in professional development can bring positive returns. Without the organizational support, the formula would look more like this:

> If satisfaction = 10, learning = 10, and organizational support = 0, then $10 \times 10 \times 0 = 0$.

Level 4: Participant Use of New Knowledge and Skills

Level 4 gets to the heart of the educator's professional practice. At this level, the evaluation enters the classroom, where application and use are assessed. This differs from Level 2 in which new learning is assessed based on some test or demonstration of the skill or knowledge in isolation. At Level 4, implementation is evaluated in terms of degree and quality. A successful professional development experience should lead to the skillful implementation, adaptation, and improvement of the new learning over time. This would require a variety of methods for assessing the implementation, including direct observations, learning team dialogues, participant reflections, structured interviews, student surveys, and video or audio documentation.

Level 5: Student Learning Outcomes

Guskey's highest level of professional development evaluation focuses on "professional development's ultimate goal: improvements in student learning outcomes" (2003, p. 750). Guskey asserts that these outcomes should include a wide variety of indicators of student performance, including achievement (test scores, grades, scholarships, and so on); behaviors (discipline referrals, meritorious actions, and so on); engagement (attendance, dropout rates, participation rates, truancy); and affective outcomes (attitudes and dispositions). These indicators can be measured using a variety of tools, including standardized tests, norm-referenced tests, teacher-developed assessments, observations, surveys, and log sheets, to name a few.

> ### Team Reflection: Evaluation and Professional Development
> *At what level is professional development evaluated in your district or school? What is one thing you can do as a team to embed the highest levels of evaluation in whatever you do?*

The potential for success is limitless when evaluation of professional development occurs at this level—when it is linked to student learning outcomes—and when the new learning consistently aligns with and supports organizational and individual professional goals.

Rethinking Professional Development

The National Staff Development Council has made it very clear that their number one priority is to help schools and districts change the way they do professional development so that it becomes much more job-embedded, collaborative, and results-oriented. We also know from extensive research conducted by the Education Trust (cited in Barth, Haycock, & Jackson, 1999) that one of the most important factors impacting student learning is teacher quality. Professional learning in schools is not a trivial matter. If we take our commitment to students seriously, we will have to stop doing professional development the old way. We will need to stop depending on single-shot workshops that expose teachers to new concepts but do nothing to help them translate that learning into practice. We will need to stop offering a smorgasbord of choices that are not aligned to the key learning needs of our students. We will need to build in more job-embedded professional learning in which teams of teachers have ongoing opportunities to share instructional practices, examine student work, visit each other's classrooms, go on field site visits together, and experience other ways to learn together while on the job, instead of only learning at a conference or workshop. We need to start aligning professional development choices with the greatest area of learning need for *students*, and we need to support teachers in planning professional learning goals that align with their SMART student learning goals. These are systemic changes requiring tremendous will and persistence, but the results for students and teachers are well worth the investment. In the next chapter, we will explore how to create capacity for this type of goal-oriented thinking in a school so that every teacher's efforts are focused, aligned, and results-oriented.

Chapter 6

Building Capacity for Goal-Oriented Thinking

"As teachers, our first step begins with a genuine desire to seek a better way of doing things, to truly believe that new paths to learning are worth exploring."

—Terry Weeks, 1988 Teacher of the Year
(cited in DuFour & Eaker, 1998, p. 231)

West High School in Madison, Wisconsin, is an excellent school by many measures. A high percentage of students go on to college and even do postgraduate work, and the school has more than its share of National Merit Scholars; however, it also has a growing number of disenfranchised, underperforming students, many of whom are poor and minority children. Five years ago, the school began to look at the achievement gap and question the reasons behind it. Social studies teacher Ginny Kester and two students successfully applied for a grant to lay the foundation for a student leadership program to address both student culture and achievement at West High School.

Kester initiated the Honor Guard program, which is aimed at developing a group of upperclassmen as leaders and tutors. Seniors in good academic standing (with an A or B average) in a subject they could tutor others in are invited to join. The Honor Guard's responsibility is to sign up for one of seven study hall ("resource hall") times, staff a study table (science, math, English, or social studies), and provide assistance to whoever comes to the table. During a training program, each Honor Guard participant is encouraged to share ideas for improvement. Kester has always stressed, "This is new territory and *we're* creating it as we go."

"To learn is to face transformation."

—Parker J. Palmer (cited in Sparks, 2003, p. 40)

During one of the resource halls, Sai, a Hmong senior, explained that when he was a freshman he had not received any help, and now through Honor Guard he could help other Hmong students who may feel left out or confused. He summed up the Honor Guard's purpose when he said proudly, "We were part of designing this and we keep improving it." Kester is tracking the program's effectiveness by working with the school's staff to monitor participating students' grades and attendance.

Among the many things that make Kester an exceptional teacher-leader is her clear, purposeful, passionate vision for ensuring that each and every student succeeds—no excuses, no matter what. Her vision has always been supported by clear goals for improvement. She will not feel her work is done until there has been dramatic improvement in the performance of students, *and* there is a system in place that will continue to support improvement. Further, she has always taken a data-driven approach to improvement, whether in analyzing student assessment results or soliciting their opinions via surveys or focus groups. In doing so, Kester is both a tremendous learner as well as a teacher-leader.

Why do some teachers take initiative while others hold back and wait to be told what to do, or even resist when invited to participate in improvement efforts? What is it about Ginny Kester that has driven her to pursue her dream of helping all kids succeed in spite of setbacks and frustrations? Are leaders like Kester born or can they be made?

It is true that individuals like Kester have particular personalities that lead them to take a world view different from those who choose not to lead. Research studies on the differences between optimists and pessimists help explain why. Martin Seligman, a psychologist at the University of Pennsylvania, has conducted some of the most powerful research on the relationship between optimism and motivation. He found that "people who are optimistic see a failure as due to something that can be changed so that they can succeed next time around, while pessimists take the blame for failure, ascribing it to some lasting characteristic they are helpless to change" (Goleman, 1995, p. 88). Pessimists tend to stop trying after a negative experience while optimists persevere. If you are a pessimist and your first experience in leading was less than positive, you may simply give up. However, there are ways to create an environment in which people like Kester will step forward and pessimistic attitudes can be reshaped. This chapter will examine the elements of effective leadership, the role of vision and goals in effective leadership, barriers to teachers taking on leadership, strategies for eliminating or reducing these barriers, and ways teachers can build leadership capacity.

"When we set a goal, we're saying, 'I can envision something different from what is, and I choose to focus my efforts to create it.' We use our imagination to keep the goal in mind, and our independent will to pay the price to achieve it."

—Stephen Covey (1994, p. 140)

The Power of Optimism

John Gardner (1986) once observed, "Every great leader is clearly teaching—and every great teacher is leading" (p. 19). The characteristics of leading and teaching are, in fact, strikingly similar: Both great teachers and great leaders possess clear vision and purpose, are effective communicators, and are willing to be judged based on results. By any standard, Ginny is both a great teacher and a great leader. But if there is one characteristic that sets her apart from those who choose not to lead it is her *belief* in her effectiveness—her conviction that there is always a better way of doing things and that she can find that way. Jim Collins (2001), whose life's work is the study of leadership, found in his research that great leaders are those "individuals who blend extreme personal humility with *professional will* [italics added]" (p. 21). Professional will is the equivalent of efficacy: When we believe in ourselves, we strive harder to find solutions, and we feel more effective when we reach them. Goals are at the heart of building this efficacy, as Stephen Covey (1994) notes:

> "When we exercise the courage to set and act on goals that are connected to principles and conscience, we tend to achieve positive results. Over time, we create an upward spiral of confidence and courage. Our commitment becomes stronger than our moods. We build the courage to set increasingly challenging, even heroic goals." (p. 152)

The context for Ginny Kester's goals is her principles and beliefs. She does not believe intelligence is immutable or set in stone, but rather that anyone can learn, grow, and change if they apply themselves. Her life experiences have convinced her of this truth; she has proven to herself that with consistent, strong support anyone can change for the better. Because she believes that everyone can learn, she takes responsibility for helping students believe in themselves through insisting that they build their skills and knowledge—even when they do not want to or see no need, which is almost always the case with underachievers at the beginning of the learning process. She sees the potential in each student, the hidden genius, and has the patience and persistence to push students until the genius emerges. At the heart of it, she is an optimist, seeing half-full glasses where others would see only half-empty ones. Goal-setting is an imminently optimistic enterprise and comes naturally to her. By setting and pursuing goals, she is saying, in essence, "I can see a future that is different from and better than the current reality, and I believe that if I invest my time and energy, I can make that future happen." Pessimists, on the other hand, see no future and no way to create a future. They feel helpless to affect change.

Individual Reflection: Challenges

Think about some challenging experiences you've had. How did you approach those experiences? Did the challenge make you want to work harder or did you give up? When is it okay to give up and when should you persevere? What role, if any, did goals play in your perseverance?

Optimism and Motivation

Martin Seligman has conducted some of the most powerful research on the relationship between optimism and motivation. Seligman's most well-known study involved insurance salespeople. He found that the optimists far outperformed the pessimists, even if they did not have the requisite sales skills and experience that the pessimists had. When the pessimists met rejection, they would interpret it as a personal failure, telling themselves, "I'm a failure at this; I'll never make a sale." Pessimists quit within the first year at twice the rate of optimists. When optimists met rejection, their attitude tended to be, "I'm using the wrong approach" or "That person was just in a bad mood" (Goleman, 1995, p. 89). They outsold pessimists by 37%. The pessimist blames himself or herself and gives up; the optimist blames the process and tries again.

Optimism and Hope

Hope plays a large role in the optimist's life, and it turns out that hope is a key resiliency skill for doing well academically. C. R. Snyder, a psychologist at the University of Kansas, conducted a study with college students that showed hope was a far better predictor of first-semester grades than SAT scores. Snyder writes, "Students with high hope set themselves higher goals and know how to work hard to attain them" (Goleman, 1991, p. 86).

Snyder goes on to say that hope is "believing you have both the will and the way to accomplish your goals, whatever they may be" (p. 87). Hopeful people, Snyder feels, share some common characteristics:

- They are able to motivate themselves.
- They feel resourceful enough to find ways to accomplish their objectives.
- They reassure themselves that things will get better when things are not going well.
- They are flexible, able to find different ways to get their goals met—or even to switch goals as needed.
- They are able to break a large task down into manageable pieces.

"To set and work toward any goal is an act of courage."

—Stephen Covey (1994, p. 152)

In citing the research on optimism, Daniel Goleman (1995), author of *Emotional Intelligence*, writes that hopeful people are less prone to depression, are persistent in the face of challenges and setbacks, and are less anxious in general. In sum, hope is all about self-efficacy—the belief that one's efforts will lead to positive results—and this in turn has powerful effects on one's health and quality of life.

Individual Reflection: Optimists and Pessimists

How do your students view themselves? Who is an optimist? Who is a pessimist? What could you do to help pessimistic students learn to become more optimistic?

Developing Competence

Can hope be learned? Can pessimists become optimists? Fortunately for students and adults alike, the answer is a resounding "Yes!" The key is to develop competence so that one has evidence of one's abilities and thereby comes to believe in oneself. Interestingly, the opposite is not true: Working on one's self-esteem will not necessarily lead to hope and optimism. Goleman (1995) writes:

> "Developing a competency of any kind strengthens the sense of self-efficacy, making a person more willing to take risks and seek out more demanding challenges. And surmounting those challenges in turn increases the sense of self-efficacy. This attitude makes people more likely to make the best use of whatever skills they may have—or do what it takes to develop them." (pp. 89–90)

This is why it is so important to work with students on clear learning targets, providing specific, timely, descriptive feedback—the assessment *for* learning approach. As students experience success with specific skills, they begin to feel smarter and are willing to try harder the next time. It is also why it is so important to build every teacher's skills in data analysis, teamwork, action research methods, leadership, and change management. When teachers begin to experience success in implementing instructional changes and see evidence of that success in their students' work and motivation, they in turn begin to feel more effective. When they experience success in implementing organizational changes at the school level and see evidence through the changed behaviors of their colleagues, they begin to feel effective as leaders of change.

Harrison High School is a great example of this cycle at work. A school improvement leadership team, composed of a principal, assistant principal, and department heads, attended the first 3 days of a 9-day training for facilitation of the SMART Schools process. Coming into the training, the team was initially cautious, even cynical. As Jamie Lipovsky, a teacher on the team later wrote, "I've been to trainings before and . . . I usually spend a lot of the training thinking about my students and strategies on how to reteach what the sub screwed up." With many opportunities during the training to practice the skills and techniques in a safe setting, team members grew in their confidence. After the training, the leadership team created a 3-day workshop for the high school staff using what they had learned, and they experienced great success. The same teacher wrote, "By the end of the 3 days, almost every staff member had the opportunity to talk to the group and present some material, and with the flurry of participation, you could kind of sense a movement occurring. . . . The response was unbelievable." One of the results of this new optimism was that the science department team finally approached the school board with some ideas they had wanted to implement for a long time. As the teacher wrote, "As a department, we have felt these changes were necessary for years, but now we have the leadership training to take the next step."

Team Reflection: Leadership Skills

What leadership skills does your team already possess? What leadership skills would your team like to learn?

Where are the opportunities for your team to exercise leadership?

How could your team help others learn leadership skills and knowledge? How could you build leadership capacity in your school?

Set at least one SMART goal for building leadership capacity.

In an interview by Daniel Goleman (1995), Stanford psychologist Albert Bandura said:

> "People's beliefs about their abilities have a profound effect on those abilities. Ability is not a fixed property; there is a huge variability in how you

perform. People who have a sense of self-efficacy bounce back from failures; they approach things in terms of how to handle them rather than worrying about what can go wrong." (p. 90)

Fortunately, self-efficacy *can* be learned and people can become more resilient in the face of adversity if, through mastering skills and seeing evidence of their hard work, they see that their efforts do pay off. Unfortunately, there is also much that conspires against teachers learning how effective they can be as leaders.

The teachers at Meadowbrook Middle School in Fort Worth, Texas, are experiencing a change in their culture—from pessimism to optimism—through the evidence of their hard work. Last year the school was placed on the state's improvement list and teachers were feeling understandably demoralized. After a year spent learning and applying the SMART Goals Process—focusing on critical learning targets, tracking student progress by zones, collaborating about instructional strategies—the staff came together to review their end-of-year data. Students showed growth in all areas based on the 2005 Panel Recommendation phase-in report, but many teachers only looked at the data from a superficial approach and felt they had not shown enough growth. However, with the realization that incremental growth had occurred, they did begin to see the light at the end of the tunnel. One teacher commented, "I came in today dreading this—I thought I'd need to find another job. By the end of the morning, I realized I know I can do this!"

Barriers to Teacher Leadership

Seymour Sarason once said, "Change depends on what teachers do and think; it's as simple and as complex as that" (cited in Fullan & Stiegelbauer, 1991, p. 117). As we have seen, what teachers do and think is very much connected to belief systems, and belief systems in turn are shaped by evidence of effectiveness as well as the degree to which a teacher is or is not an optimist. There are a variety of reasons, however, that teachers may not take the risk of becoming goal-oriented leaders, even if they are optimists. One key reason is that norms and expectations for collaboration and improvement are often not well developed. Traditional school norms are isolationist, preventing collaboration and involvement. These norms are supported by a "manufacturing production mentality"—a leftover from the early 1900s when Frederick Taylor's ideas reigned supreme—emphasizing face-to-face student time and little or no collaborative improvement planning time. In a production mentality school, one person is in charge (the principal) and the rest are the "doers" (the teachers). There is no reason for shared vision and values since one person is making all the decisions. Without shared vision and values, there is no context for goal-setting. The result is unfortunate: Student achievement tends to be either static or on a downward spiral. As Linda Lambert (2002) notes, "The old model of formal, one person leadership leaves the substantial talents of teachers largely untapped. Improvements achieved under this model are not easily sustainable" (p. 37).

Another reason teachers may not take initiative lies in their not having had the opportunity to hone their critical thinking skills. Critical thinking skills—the ability to organize, summarize, synthesize, analyze, draw conclusions, make generalizations, and inferences—are critical to leadership. Carl Glickman (1993) argues that:

> "Teachers with high abstract thinking skills can view the problem from many perspectives (their own, students', parents', aides', administrators') and can generate many alternative solutions. They can think through the advantages and disadvantages of each plan and decide upon the most promising one. They are willing to change that plan if the predicted consequences do not materialize." (p. 86)

Since "high abstract thinking skills" are the ones that students tend to be weakest in, it should come as no surprise that many teachers, products of our public education system, may not have had much experience in this area. If you are not accustomed to thinking about problems at high levels of complexity, it is doubtful that you will see the depth and breadth of a situation and know what to do about it.

A final reason teachers may not engage in leadership is that past implementation of change initiatives may have significantly underestimated the time required and overestimated the benefits that would accrue. Those involved in the change effort may have been inadequately prepared. As Fullan and Stiegelbauer (1991) observe, "personal costs in time, energy, and threat to sense of adequacy, with no evidence of benefit in return, seem to have constituted the major costs of changes in education over the past 30 years" (p. 128). No one likes to feel inadequate or incompetent; indeed, we will go to great lengths to avoid the embarrassment of failure. Many so-called resistors or nonleaders may in fact have simply invested significant energy in change processes in the past with poor or inadequate results and are now choosing to "sit it out." If they are pessimistic by nature, chances are they see the failure as personal and are not willing to try again. Unfortunately, these people get labeled as deadwood. But as Fullan notes, "By far the main problem in teaching is not how to get rid of the deadwood, but rather how to motivate good teachers throughout their careers. *Changes in the culture of teaching and the culture of schools are required* [italics added]" (p. 143). Since motivation is not a matter of "what I can get you to do," but "what you choose to commit to," the culture of the school and its support for teacher leadership clearly have a significant impact on reengaging the deadwood as well as all others.

When teachers are not given the opportunity to lead, when they do not have the skills and resources to lead, or when they have had negative experiences with leading in the past, it is highly likely they will not see themselves as leaders and therefore will not engage in change. If they are pessimists on top of that, it is doubtful that they will persist in taking initiative for leadership when faced with cultural norms that perpetuate isolationism and the status quo.

Team Reflection: Confidence Building

Dr. Rick Stiggins believes that if a student has given up, it can take up to 20 to 30 instances of successful learning experiences to rebuild his or her confidence. If a teacher has given up, how many successful leadership experiences do you think it would take to rebuild his or her confidence? What actions might be taken to rebuild this confidence?

Strategies for Reducing—or Eliminating—the Barriers

Most researchers and educational leaders agree that the principal is the key person for creating cultural change at the school level. Even though, as Lambert says, "leadership is the professional work of everyone in the school" (p. 37), the principal is the primary initiator in creating a school where everyone learns and everyone leads. The principal's belief system is the foundation for the kind of leadership the staff experiences. Combs, Miser, and Whitaker (1999) write, "What you believe about the nature of people and their motivation in life has far reaching consequences for how you approach leadership tasks and relationships" (p. 47).

Working From Our Beliefs

If as a principal you believe that teachers are more interested in their contracts than their students, that they are not very bright and come to work looking for ways to get out of work, that shared leadership is just another word for anarchy, then you will employ what Combs, Miser, and Whitaker (1999) call a "things-oriented manipulative" approach. You will establish norms of control, compliance, and inspection. You will be uncomfortable releasing leadership to others, and you will do little to create leadership opportunities. You may talk about leadership capacity building, but your actions will communicate top-down, hierarchical control. The result will be what psychologists call learned helplessness behavior on the part of teachers—behavior that is dependent and passive. This in turn will reinforce your belief that teachers really cannot and should not lead.

However, if you believe that people are good, that they come to work wanting to do a good job, and that your job is to release their inner genius, you will approach your work as a staff developer—much as Ginny Kester approaches her work with her students. You will establish a climate of trust, norms of high expectations, and a crystal clear vision of teaching, learning, and leadership. You will continually work with staff, students, parents, and community leaders to create a shared vision for the future of the school and to create clear values to guide behaviors and actions toward that vision. You will build your staff members' confidence in their leadership skills by modeling these skills and facilitative behaviors yourself, and by meta-cognitively talking about what you are doing, why you are doing it, and how you are doing it. You will coach your staff in using these skills, providing the scaffolding they need until they are ready to lead on their own. You will provide many opportunities for leadership, from involvement on the school improvement leadership team, to study circles, to action research teams, to SMART goals teams at the grade and department levels, and other leadership venues. Above all, you will see your job as creating the environment where people feel "I can" versus "I can't"—the same environment you expect teachers to create in their classrooms.

Sandy Gunderson, principal of Mendota Elementary School in Madison, Wisconsin, believes that "first you have to believe in the child and then he will believe in himself." A corollary principle that Gunderson operates from each and every day is that first the teacher must believe in him- or herself; then he or she can believe in the child. She sees her job as "bringing out the best in every employee." She builds a sense of efficacy in each and every teacher so that these teachers in turn build efficacy in their students. In the early years of the school's improvement journey, she went to every grade-level team meeting. She modeled effective meeting skills, coached the teachers in how to align their standards with assessments and in how to analyze student results, and mentored teachers in developing effective communication and conflict-management skills. Along with her Title 1 school-wide facilitator, she worked with each team to develop SMART goals aligned with the school's improvement goals. Seven years ago Mendota, with 50% poverty and high mobility, had some of the worst test scores in the city. There were many union grievances, student suspensions, and parent complaints to the board. Even though today Mendota has a 70% poverty rate, the school is at the top of the district in both climate and achievement.

Five years into their improvement journey, Sandy Gunderson had to be hospitalized and was out of school for 6 weeks. There were no emergencies that required a call to her and no big problems to resolve when she returned. The school ran smoothly and effectively while she was gone, and the teachers even initiated some new changes. Her belief in the staff and her willingness to invest her personal time and energy in growing their competence as leaders resulted in strong leadership capacity. This challenging situation illustrates just how far the staff came in a relatively short period of time and just how much teacher leadership capacity had been built in the school. Today Gunderson says, "These teachers are awesome! Now I just get out of their way."

Sandy Gunderson is practicing the type of leadership that Deborah Wortham, principal of an elementary school in Baltimore, Maryland, spoke about when she called on school leaders to "feed teachers" emotionally and professionally. At an ASCD teaching and learning conference in 2003, keynote speaker Wortham exhorted leaders to "celebrate their successes and cultivate their leadership qualities." True leaders reproduce, she observed: they "make other people great."

The National Staff Development Council recognizes that for principals to grow teacher leadership, they will have to learn new skills and attitudes themselves. This will require principals to think about their role differently, to evaluate their own belief systems, and to build their own skillfulness as facilitative leaders. NSDC's leaders write that principals:

"Must learn how to build support for change, motivate teachers to become leaders and take charge of their own projects, and provide reasons for people to want to change. They need to learn how to let go of some authority and controls so teachers also have opportunities to become leaders." (2000, p. 15)

Effective leaders operate from a belief system of empowerment. They build on strengths, seeing teachers as "intellectual rather than teacher as technician" (Little, 1993, p. 129). They encourage teachers to make choices, but within a structure and process founded in the continuous improvement philosophy. They provide many opportunities for collaboration and teamwork, and they support the growing leadership skills of their teachers. Effective leaders encourage peer coaching, reflective inquiry, and collaborative action research. They provide opportunities for teachers to grow in their effectiveness as teachers. But they do not stop there. They also support their growth as effective leaders, providing many opportunities to lead and supporting them with coaching and feedback. Their vision is that each and every staff member is a learner who is able to lead with confidence and competence. Their goal is to build that competence teacher by teacher, team by team. In the final analysis, when that leader leaves the school, the building is able to sustain continuous improvement and learning through the leadership capacity that has become institutionalized.

Five Things Principals Can Do to Grow Teacher Leadership

1. *Model leadership skills and behavior. Listen respectfully, facilitate conversations and meetings skillfully, and encourage participation.*

2. *Use inquiry skills. Ask more than you tell.*

3. *Expect the best in people. Confront mediocrity.*

4. *Give specific, nonjudgmental feedback.*

5. *Find the good and praise it.*

Restructuring Time

To encourage teacher leadership, principals need to create an environment in which that leadership will emerge and flourish. To do so will require improvements to the structure of the school day and year—improvements that will provide time for collaborative reflection and action planning. Time, the most valuable resource in schools, will need to be reallocated so that teachers can think about their goals, gather evidence of progress on their goals, and make adjustments to their strategies based on that evidence. Currently many schools are structured, at best, for 95% production time (student face-to-face time, lesson planning, grading, and so on) and only 5% of time for collaborative reflection and improvement. Given that successful businesses devote 20% of time to improvement work and planning, schools have a long way to go! Teachers know this is a problem: The number one thing they complain about is lack of time to reflect on implementation of changes. Fortunately there are countless examples of ways schools have made time for improvement (late starts, early dismissals, block scheduling, and so on); we are limited only by our human ingenuity and our will to make the necessary changes. Initiative for this may come from teacher-leaders, but it is the principal who decides whether structural changes will be implemented.

Building Optimism

Research on optimism and pessimism indicates that pessimism can be unlearned through a combination of successful experiences and self-talk, the words we say to ourselves internally that have the power to either encourage us to keep going or give up. As an example, in one 12-week study, Seligman coached 10- to 13-year-olds who showed signs of depression. The result was that "they learned some basic emotional skills, including handling disagreements, thinking before acting, and perhaps most important, *challenging the pessimistic beliefs* [italics added] associated with depression" (Goleman, 1995, p. 246). Seligman and his associates helped the children reframe their self-talk while they learned new skills. In the same way, principals can play a powerful role in helping pessimistic teachers reframe their self-talk while learning new leadership skills. Leading change is essentially managing one conversation at a time; reframing the conversation is a key skill and will require great empathy for how teachers are feeling (just as we feel empathy for our students) while insisting that teachers try again.

Peter Senge believes schools tend to operate out of negative mental models, in which "the whole system is focused on fixing kids" (1990, p. 45). Senge continues, "When we're solving problems, we're trying to get rid of things we don't want." The work of continually focusing on getting rid of what we do not want requires tremendous energy, leaving us feeling exhausted—what author and master teacher Parker Palmer calls "bad tired"—at the end of the day. In the same way, if principals focus solely on getting rid of deadwood, they will feel de-energized by day's end. What if the focus instead was on finding what each person is good at and helping them do more of it, in order to build their confidence and competence? At Jenifer Junior High School in Lewiston, Idaho, Bob Donaldson does exactly that.

As a principal, Donaldson believes that "when you expect the best in people, they live up to it." He works hard to find out what people are good at and gets them to take leadership in that area. His philosophy is to "plant the seed and then step back." For example, several years ago he asked, "What if we opened up our school at night for our students and parents?" A small group of teachers with experience coordinating workshops then came to him with ideas for running "Parent Nights." Two years ago, Parent Nights drew only 20 attendees, most of whom were staff. Today, Parent Nights are held every 3 weeks, with as many as 300 people attending, most of them parents and students.

Sometimes expecting the best in people means pushing them out of their comfort zones. The school's athletic director, for example, was dead set against implementing "no cut" sports. However, Donaldson felt strongly, based on the research, that developmentally a "no cut" policy would be best for kids. He insisted that the director find a way to make "no cut" work, telling him, "I know you can make this work because I have confidence in you and I know how much you care about the kids." Several months later, the athletic director came to Donaldson to tell him how excited he was about the changes he had seen in the students as a result of the new policy. "This has been the best thing that could have happened to kids," he said. "In fact, it's the best I've seen in 30 years of coaching." Donaldson has created a strong team culture in his school where teachers initiate change and innovation based on their research. Those who are unwilling to embrace change are confronted but also given support and encouragement.

Principals also encourage goal-focused leadership when they recognize and celebrate this behavior publicly. One of the key principles of building a strong professional learning community is to recognize progress and celebrate improvement. Doing this publicly communicates the idea that "this is what is valued here— this is what is important." When Rick DuFour was principal at Adlai Stevenson High School, he began a tradition of telling stories about individual teachers in the school that illustrated the type of student-centered, innovative leadership he was looking for in the rest of the staff. He encouraged teachers to come forward and tell stories about their colleagues, and this continues as a standard feature of all faculty meetings. The practice is powerful not only because it resonates with the storyteller in all of us, but because it communicates cultural norms and values even more convincingly than is possible in one-on-one conversations.

Peter Senge encourages us to focus on what we want rather than just fixing what is going wrong. He says, "When we're creating, we are bringing into reality things that are valued by us" (Sparks, 2001, p. 45). This is goal-directed leadership: identifying a vision of the future and establishing goals for accomplishing that vision. When principals work with teachers to define that vision and those goals, and then support them in building competencies so they can achieve the goals, they break the cycle of negativism, cynicism, and apathy that can be so dysfunctional in a school. Principals who actively engage teachers in reflective inquiry, helping them constantly reflect on their students' work in the context of their goals, will help teachers make a sustained commitment to the school's vision, values, and goals. As their expertise deepens and expands, they will begin to feel more effective and will, in turn, put more effort into goal-directed behavior. As Michael Fullan writes, "when the changes involve a sense of mastery, excitement, and accomplishment, the incentives for trying new practices are powerful" (Fullan & Stiegelbauer, 1991, pp. 128–129). For our purposes, new practices include both instructional practices and leadership skills. At the end of the day, a principal who has worked on creating mastery among his or her teachers will go home feeling "good tired" instead of "bad tired."

What Teachers Can Do to Build Leadership

Any teacher can—and should—become a leader. The question is what type of leader? We all know of highly dysfunctional schools with plenty of toxic leaders—not what is needed if all students are to succeed. What is needed is a clear vision of *effective* leadership. The first step for a teacher is to define that vision. What does an effective leader look like? What are the characteristics? What does an ineffective leader look like? Once that clear vision is in place, the next step is to push the mental model of leadership further, beyond the parameters of traits and characteristics. What is leadership if it is not a person? Linda Lambert writes:

> "Leadership is broader than the sum total of its leaders, for it also involves an energy flow or synergy generated by those who choose to lead. It is this wave of energy and purpose that engages and pulls others into the work of leadership." (1998, p. 5)

Individual Reflection: Energy Flow

Think of a time when you felt the kind of energy flow Lambert talks about. How did that feel? Who was leading? What did leading look like?

Team Reflection: Teacher Leadership

What do we think of teacher leadership now? What assumptions do we hold? What experiences have we had?

If leadership is energy flow, what is the responsibility of the teacher-leader in creating, developing, and sustaining that flow?

Leadership as an energy flow is a much richer definition than the traditional trait-based model. It gives us permission not to have to be charismatic or strong or superorganized—all traditional characteristics of effective leaders. It opens the door for all to engage in leadership as an ongoing practice in our schools. This does not mean we should not be developing ourselves as effective leaders, but it does challenge us to see our role differently—more as builders of others' leadership than as "take-charge" leaders.

The research is very clear that schools with strong leadership capacity do better than schools without that capacity (Newmann, King, & Youngs, 1999). Lambert (1998) defines leadership capacity as broad-based, skillful participation in the creation and fulfillment of a vision focused on student learning. High leadership capacity schools are characterized by many opportunities for everyone to engage in leadership; everyone sharing high levels of skillfulness in leadership; coordinated, aligned programs and activities; and a constant focus on improvement. The question for the emerging teacher-leader is this: "What can I do to contribute to building leadership capacity in my school?" Lambert (2003) outlines specific benchmarks teachers can attend to that will grow not only their own leadership, but also grow leadership capacity in the school. Teachers should:

- Initiate new action by suggesting other ways to accomplish tasks or goals.

- Solve problems instead of asking permission and assigning blame.

- Volunteer to take responsibility for issues or tasks.

- Invite other teachers to work with them, share materials, and visit classrooms.

- Listen to each other, and particularly to new members of the staff.

- Admit to mistakes and unsolved instructional issues, and ask for assistance from colleagues.

- Talk about children in a way that suggests that all children can learn.

- Become more skillful in conversations, facilitation, asking questions, and teaching.

When these benchmarks are used to develop SMART goals, they become powerful motivators for moving toward the vision of effective leadership and leadership capacity building. A teacher could commit to a SMART goal such as "By the end of this year, I will take responsibility for one initiative that will have school-wide implications" or "This quarter I will apply two reflective inquiry skills—surfacing assumptions and digging into causes—in my meetings as appropriate."

The Power of Reflection

People who engage in reflective practice tend to have a quiet, steady, very calming presence. Their thoughts seem to come from a deeper, more analytical place, and they are often able to slow conversations down to a pace where everyone is thinking more deeply and reflectively. Author and master teacher Parker Palmer has just this presence. When you meet him, his eyes look straight into yours, taking you in completely. When you speak together, he questions more than he tells, and he listens intently to your responses. His observations are deep, thoughtful, honest, human, and always illuminating. You come away from these meetings feeling renewed, refreshed, and ready to take on the next challenge. Parker is a model of what effective leading looks like. A large part of why he is so effective is the amount of time he spends in contemplation, thinking, and writing.

Engaging in reflection is one of the most powerful things teachers can do to grow their leadership; however, contemplation and reflection are rare in schools. As Roland Barth (2001) writes, "I find the life of a school person akin to that of a tennis shoe in a laundry dryer—congested, convoluted, lumpy, dark, endless" (p. 38). These are hardly conditions conducive to reflective practice, but reflection is where we find the inner knowledge to seek goals that are meaningful and to solve problems at deep levels. As Barth says, "Learning from experience is not inevitable. It must be intentional" (p. 38). He makes an important distinction between reflecting *in* and reflecting *on* practice, commenting that reflecting *in* is like trying to reflect while you are in the middle of the laundry dryer or in the middle of the work day. Reflecting *on* is reflecting outside of the dryer, outside of the work day, and involves written reflection. "In order to know what I think," Barth believes, "I have to write and see what I say" (p. 39). Stephen Covey would agree with this, observing that we add far more power to the goals when we add conscience and self-awareness to goal-setting.

How can we begin this written reflective practice as we work on leadership goals? Covey suggests starting with "the end in mind." First, identify *what* you want to accomplish. This is your goal, and it should focus on growth and contribution. It is very much connected to your mission and vision. Second, identify *why* you want to accomplish your goal, what the key drivers are. Are you driven by your principles, by a need, or by your mission in life? The importance of the "why" cannot be understated. As

---

Ways Teachers Can Lead

Teachers can…

- *Serve on governance committees*

- *Mentor less experienced staff*

- *Coach peers*

- *Support colleagues who want to seek certification through the National Board for Professional Teaching Standards*

- *Serve on faculty committees that make key decisions for the school*

- *Participate in lesson studies*

- *Serve on a school improvement team to create school improvement plans and professional development programs*

- *Share skills formally and informally with new teachers*

- *Discuss formally and informally ways the school can be improved*

- *Participate in action research*

(National Staff Development Council, 2000, p. 8)

Covey says, "The key to motivation is motive. It's the 'why.' It's what gives us the energy to stay strong in hard moments. It gives us the strength to say 'no' because we connect with a deeper 'yes!' burning inside" (1994, p. 142).

Once you have a clear "why," you are ready for the *how*, identifying the key strategies you will employ to achieve your goal, and the principles and values that will help guide your way. In addition, it is important to consider the evidence we will accept as progress on our goal. How will we know? How will we measure? What evidence will we look for?

Bringing intentionality to our goal-setting through written reflective practice is key to sustaining our vision as teacher-leaders. It slows us down enough that we contemplate our goals, evaluate our progress, and make adjustments. Reflection truly is at the heart of continuous improvement.

Teachers Need to Collaborate

Another thing teachers can do to grow their leadership skills is to find other teachers who are leaders and wish to collaborate. There is nothing lonelier and more disheartening than being the proverbial "petunia in an onion patch." A personal story illustrates how important it is to get out of that patch and find other petunias.

When Jan first began teaching, she was surrounded by well-meaning non-leaders. She was ready to quit after only 2 years of teaching because she felt so isolated and incompetent. Fortunately she discovered late in the year a kindred spirit: a veteran teacher who shared her same ideals and goals. They successfully lobbied the administration to allow team teaching the following year. Jan learned more that year about leadership and good instruction than she had learned in all her coursework, student teaching, and early teaching experiences. As a result of that experience, she was able to find her voice: She began speaking up more confidently in meetings and was asked to serve on a district committee. In retrospect, she would say the experience moved her from a pessimistic to an optimistic outlook and helped her begin to see herself as both an effective teacher and an effective leader.

When teachers of like minds work together, they can create tremendous movement for positive change. Ginny Kester's ability to create big changes in her high school was fueled in large part by the supportive team of teachers who have come together to create a professional learning community culture. Linda Lambert (2003) writes, "Teacher leaders are those whose dreams of making a difference have either been kept alive or have been reawakened by engaging with colleagues and working within a professional culture" (p. 33). Kester's dream of making a difference has always been active, but with a support group, she was able to go farther than she could ever have gone before. As the saying goes, "Don't preach to the choir and don't preach to the casket. Preach to the congregation!" Leadership is a courageous and not always appreciated act, so it is also important to spend some time with the choir, get re-energized, and recommit to your original vision and goals.

"Far too many teams casually accept goals that are neither demanding, precise, realistic, nor actually held in common. . . . Teamwork alone never makes a team."

—J. R. Kantzenback and K. D. Smith (1993)

A Clear Vision of Student Success

It is the right and the responsibility of each of us to lead in our schools. However, as teachers we will need to become more self-aware and more intentional about our roles as teacher-leaders if we are to have significant impact on student learning. We need to develop our will to lead through identifying a clear vision of leadership and clear goals for getting there. We need to develop our skills to lead through practicing, reflecting, and dialoguing with our colleagues. Ideally, we need environments that value us and take advantage of our leadership skills and will. However, strongly goal-oriented, optimistic people like Ginny Kester will still take initiative even in less than ideal settings because their vision of all students succeeding is so strong that even an unsupportive culture cannot hold them back.

Chapter 7

Case Studies

"Play for more than you can afford to lose, then you will learn the game."

—Winston Churchill (cited in Hobson, 1999, p. 43)

In this book we have attempted to show that many facets of professional practice are positively influenced and enhanced by the use of SMART goals. SMART goals work, and the strategies, tools, and examples presented in this book support that point. As often is the case, however, simply knowing they work is not enough. The reader is left with the nagging question, "But how can we make it happen in our school?"

What follows is a sampling of how schools at different levels and in very different circumstances have approached the introduction, implementation, and support of SMART goals in their schools. These case studies highlight the need for schools to make SMART goals their own, while adhering to some basic principles of the change process:

- Strong leadership and leadership capacity

- Data-driven decision-making

- Collaborative processes and cultures

- Goals set within the context of a shared vision

- Entire schools focused on improving student learning

We applaud the courageous leadership exhibited by the principals and teachers whose stories are told here. They are the true pioneers of reform in our education system.

Jenifer Junior High School, Lewiston, Idaho

Lewiston, Idaho, is a rural mill town with a population of slightly more than 30,000. Jenifer Junior High School is one of 12 public schools in the Lewiston district. It serves 635 seventh through ninth graders, approximately 35% of which are students of low-socioeconomic status (SES); twenty percent are identified for special education services.

Until 1993, when Bob Donaldson took over as principal, the school was departmentalized as a traditional junior high school. Test scores were generally low. On the Iowa Test of Basic Skills (ITBS), reading was at the 45th percentile, language at the 51st, and mathematics at the 46th percentile. The scores fell into a bimodal distribution with the low-socioeconomic status students consistently scoring on the lowest end of the continuum. Additionally, suspensions were very high, reaching a total of 295 in the 1995–1996 school year.

Prior to his appointment as principal, Donaldson served as assistant principal of the school. He had been unhappy with the culture and the school's performance for a long time. In his new role, he was finally able to ask the question, "Are we where we want to be?" That question started the journey of rethinking the junior high model and provided the impetus for moving toward a middle school model that was team-based and developmentally appropriate for seventh and eighth grade (ninth grade is still departmentalized).

The Middle School Model

The middle school philosophy provided a perfect opportunity for self-directed change and was formally adopted after a year of studying the options. Staff had to determine how to get started with the transformation, as there were no additional resources to fund the change.

Students were moved into appropriate physical spaces that would accommodate team teaching, advisory time, exploratory courses, and both team and individual preparation time for teachers. The way the school interacted with students and parents was completely rethought. The school culture went from a largely punitive discipline model to one committed to building positive relationships.

All stakeholders were involved in planning and implementing programs and strategies based on this new philosophy. Teachers, custodians, secretaries, education assistants—all had an opportunity to help answer the question, "What can we do to help kids feel like they are part of this school community?" One solution was to implement lunch and after-school activities that were run by multiple stakeholders. This gave everyone a chance to contribute to the new approach and to build better relationships with the students.

By year two, the staff was reorganized into teams. Little team training was available except what the principal and local university instructors were able to provide. A key component of the philosophy, teacher-student advisory time, began in this year. But because there was no designated time during the day, advisory sessions were held before and after school. This strategy did not work well because students wanted to leave at the end of day. It became clear that teachers were also going to need extra planning time, a reality that brought union action into the mix.

In the school's third year of the change process, the board allocated an additional 4.5 FTE (Full Time Equivalent), which allowed teachers more common planning time. The school hired more special area teachers (such as teachers to staff exploratory courses in health, writing, visual arts, vocational skills, computer science, and so on), added electives, and developed interdisciplinary units. The schedule was eventually revised to incorporate 90-minute teaching blocks. This decision was not made via a democratic vote. Instead, Donaldson asked, "How much additional time do students need to learn?" That question kept everyone focused on what was needed to improve student learning—the primary reason for making the change in the first place. As a result, the school moved to embedded blocks of curriculum that included a daily advisory time, daily exploratory time, and deeper, more integrated lessons in all of the content areas. There were several unexpected benefits as well. Transition time between classes was reduced, teacher planning time increased, and more "hands on" lessons were developed. Teachers now say they would not go back to the old way of doing things.

Goal-Setting

Goal-setting eventually became an important part of the process, but not until after some of the initial changes took hold. It began in the late 1990s as part of the Northwest Association accreditation process, which required schools to look at their mission, goals, and data, and to develop action plans. That helped the school become organized around its new mission and goals; however, Principal Donaldson knew that it was not enough to simply require the school staff to develop mission and goal statements. If the mission and goals were going to be instruments of change, they would need to be nurtured, not by him alone, but by everyone in the school. Initially, he saw his role as "planting the seed" and then encouraging teams to develop toward their goals. He stepped in as needed to remove obstacles and barriers, provided many articles for staff to read, and periodically checked in with teams to see what they were learning.

Ongoing support now comes in the form of regular meetings between the principal and the team leaders. The role of team leader rotates on a quarterly basis giving everyone a chance to build and exercise his or her leadership skills. Donaldson coaches the new leaders to help them become comfortable in their new role and provides them with templates for planning their agendas and for reporting on their meeting outcomes. The templates provide a standard reporting format for the teams, making it easier to document their meetings and to keep track of their decisions. Examples of similar team meeting templates can be found in *The Handbook for SMART School Teams* (Conzemius & O'Neill, 2002), page 70 and pages 281–285.

As a way to sustain and continue to grow relationships, Donaldson visits with the teams at the end of each week to informally check in and connect with the members on a personal level by asking about their weekend plans and finding out how they are feeling. He also uses these opportunities to smooth out any differences of opinion between himself and staff members that may have surfaced during the week.

Each team has its own personality and set of initiatives. For example, the seventh-grade team has a unique student-led conference system. Twice a year, the teachers set up a big conference room with separate tables where students and parents meet to discuss their learning goals. The students use goal sheets that outline their specific learning targets. Parents are given colored cards designating a particular content area. When a parent has a question for a teacher, he or she simply holds up the card. Otherwise, the students direct the conference entirely themselves. Afterward, the parents write their child a letter, which is followed by a teacher-led debriefing session. According to Donaldson, "We couldn't have done this 6 years ago—we weren't ready."

The results so far are promising. By 1998–1999 suspension rates had dropped 73%, down to 50 per year (from a high of 295 in 1995–1996), and have stayed consistent since then. Academically, the school has made steady improvement. In 1998–1999 reading was at the 67th percentile, language at the 59th, and math at the 60th. By the end of the 2004–2005 school year, 80% of all students were proficient in language, 89% were proficient in reading, and 78% were proficient in math. In addition both special education and free- and reduced-lunch students are making gains: In 2004 only 18% of special education students were proficient in reading and math. In 2005, 50% were proficient in reading, 24% in math, and 31% in language usage. In 2004, 62% of free- and reduced-lunch students were proficient in reading, 47% in math, and 66% in language. In 2005 they were in the 78th percentile proficient in reading, 63% in math, and 66% in language. The staff was proud to be recognized in 2005 as both a Merit School and a School of Excellence.

Principal Donaldson believes in the power of relationships and the power of shared goals to sustain the energy level needed to keep on improving. "We're like a person with a weight problem. We can't afford to go off our diet. We have to go out and work hard on relationships every day. When you expect the best in people, they live up to it. People come with strengths. They don't get up in the morning saying, 'I'm going to be a jerk today!' I work with their strengths; try to find places for them to shine in our school." One of the best, unanticipated outcomes of this philosophy is that almost all staff members have stayed over the years. They are a very close knit group who work well together and enjoy doing so, which provides stability, safety, and consistency for everyone in the school.

"Each year I remind the staff to be good to each other and to celebrate our accomplishments. We are making a difference. Collectively, our power to make a positive impact is limitless!"

—Bob Donaldson

Despite their tremendous progress, the journey is not always easy. Jenifer's school district has been cited by the state for not meeting adequate yearly progress (AYP) for special education students. This is difficult, but Donaldson is not worried. He reminds his staff of what they are capable of accomplishing when they share a common commitment to a student-learning goal. They have evidence of their resiliency and their skills to bring about improvement in their school. Just as this current journey began with a question, the next one will as well. Donaldson has asked the entire staff to ponder, "What does a Blue Ribbon school look like? What will it take us to get there?"

Longfellow Middle School, La Crosse, Wisconsin

"As a matter of fact . . ." is something you would hear Principal Glen Jenkins say in response to an inquiry about his school. Driven by a need to know the truth, Jenkins began looking at student and school performance data long before it was popular to do so. He calls it "managing by fact." It is Jenkins' personal desire to learn that led to a series of collaborative, school-wide improvements at Longfellow Middle School.

The city of La Crosse, Wisconsin, with a population of just over 50,000, is situated on the eastern banks of the Mississippi River in west central Wisconsin. This medium-sized, urban town includes manufacturing, recreational, and cultural opportunities. It is home to a state university, several private colleges, and world-class health care and medical research facilities.

The School District of La Crosse is composed of 21 schools—11 elementary, 3 middle, 2 high schools, and 5 charter schools—that serve the city and surrounding areas with a total population of approximately 80,000 people. Longfellow Middle School serves 637 children in grades six through eight. Whereas the district as a whole is 20% racial and ethnic minority, Longfellow's student population is closer to 10% minority. Twenty-five percent of Longfellow's students are on free- and reduced-lunch programs, compared with 28% district-wide.

Principal Jenkins started his pursuit into school improvement out of sheer frustration. He noticed that there were a multitude of initiatives that were being tried or suggested, some by the central office and others by the teachers themselves. These initiatives would be implemented for a short time until the next new idea came along. Not only were staff members feeling overwhelmed, but no one knew whether these initiatives were making any difference at all when it came to student learning.

Examining the Data

When he first began looking at the data, Jenkins noticed an unusually high failure rate. There were very significant differences in the grading process from one classroom to the next and from one grade level to the next. The number of students being recommended for retention was sky-rocketing, as were referrals for discipline and incidences of bullying. Achievement, as measured on nationally normed tests, was generally acceptable—most students were scoring between the 60th and 80th percentile. Even though the failure rates were high, no one was particularly concerned about the school's academic performance. Everyone did agree, however, that there were too many discipline referrals and that something needed to be done about the growing number of students who were disrupting the learning environment.

In the late 1980s, Jenkins launched an action research project that would ultimately take him and the Longfellow staff on a journey of change that no one would have believed possible. It began with his curiosity about three questions that he saw in the initial analysis of data:

1. To what extent do the differences in grading from one staff person to the next and from one grade level to the next impede our ability to make school-wide improvements?

2. What is the long-term impact on students who have been retained for a year at Longfellow Middle School?

3. Though our average achievement on standardized tests is acceptable, are there sub-populations of students whose performance is not acceptable? Who are these students?

After gathering data directed at each of these questions, Jenkins graphed the results and shared them with grade-level departments and with individual teachers. He then developed an all-school profile including:

- Demographic facts

- Information on families

- Standardized test scores from the early 1980s to the present

- Office and behavioral referrals

- Parent, staff, and student perceptions on the Seven Correlates of Effective Schools (Lezotte & McKee, 2002)

- Disaggregated test scores based on free- and reduced-lunch counts

The Outcomes

Here is what they learned: The differences in grading were real. They reflected a disparate, unconnected set of expectations and processes for assessing student work. There was little to no alignment of standards with marked differences in how curriculum and instruction were being designed and delivered. How can a school with so little consistency in its core functions systematically implement improvements? More importantly, how can a school know whether lasting improvements have been made when there is no common set of expectations, no common way to measure progress, and no consistent way to communicate what learning has occurred and how well?

The retention data were also very telling. Longfellow's findings mirrored what is found in the research on retention: It does not work in the long-term (Johnson & Rudolph, 2001). During the year of retention, academic performance improved for most students who were retained. Thereafter, student performance declined each year until the students were ultimately back to their original achievement levels or, in some cases, at levels reflecting even more severe achievement gaps than before being retained. Retention is a short-term, Band-Aid approach to improvement with little or no lasting benefits.

With regard to the third question, the disaggregated data revealed serious achievement gaps for low-SES students. Test scores for the middle- and high-SES students were above state and district norms, but those for the low-SES students were below state and district norms. These findings were especially unsettling to the teachers, as well as to Jenkins. The staff had always prided itself in being good and responsive to the needs of all students, but the data were not showing this. Something needed to be done.

The Steps

They began to take steps quickly and simultaneously. As analyses of the whole school's data occurred, a new configuration of school options was emerging. More variation, not less, was being introduced on a school-wide basis. In 1991, "School on the River" opened its doors. This fully-integrated curriculum for seventh- and eighth-grade students uses the river and its natural ecosystem as a learning laboratory for the school. By the mid-1990s, Longfellow Middle School had four distinct configurations of schools-within-a-school. This made the school-wide focus even more important for two reasons.

First, parents needed to be assured that their child would be held to the same high standards and expectations as any other child in the school, regardless of the unique philosophy or approach to instruction. Mission alignment, common assessments, and standards were essential means for holding the system accountable for high performance school-wide.

The second reason this consistency was so important had more to do with the adults in the school. As new school configurations were being introduced, a new level of competitiveness began to emerge. Jenkins turned to the data again, this time in the form of a perceptual survey that assessed staff, student, and parent satisfaction. The data revealed an uncomfortable degree of competition among staff members that was characterized in some cases by blaming and in other cases by accusations of favoritism.

In general, there was a lack of confidence among staff members in each other as professionals.

Trained in both the Baldridge National Quality Program (see the National Institute of Standards and Technology for more information: www.quality.nist.gov/index.html) and QLD models for continuous improvement, Jenkins began by having the staff work on a school-wide mission statement. They needed to "get on the same page" before they could move forward collectively. Jenkins recalls, "This meant people had to talk to each other—a lot. This was a very important first step because it created a common language across all school configurations." Teachers could see that even though their school's approach to learning may be very unique, they were all there for the same reason: success in student learning. The learning community had begun to form.

With Jenkins' guidance, the entire staff began to look at their data more closely. After careful consideration of several sources of data (standardized, norm-referenced tests, grades, and exams to name a few), two greatest areas of need (GAN) emerged: writing and mathematics. The findings were extremely useful in getting the staff focused, but the level of analysis needed to go deeper before they could determine what to do to improve.

For math, the staff used a final exam in their program as a pre- and post-assessment. They found that at every grade level, knowledge of math facts was weak. Could this be a gap in the curriculum? When they examined their curriculum, they indeed found that more needed to be done to engage children in learning and using their math facts. Interestingly, this was a finding that was repeated throughout the entire district. Thus, grade-level activities were developed to strengthen knowledge of math facts district-wide.

In the area of writing, Longfellow staff engaged in a two-and-a-half year process to:

- Define writing

- Agree on grade-level expectations for student performance

- Share instructional strategies such as, "How do you teach writing a paragraph?"

- Pre- and post-test all students using a common writing rubric developed by the staff

- Analyze and interpret their data in light of instructional strategies

This process included a combination of dialogue, sharing best practices, collaborative inquiry, and problem solving. It turned out to be a powerful confidence builder among the staff and a means for further developing their common mission—even in light of their different instructional approaches.

SMART Goals and Action Plans

Another powerful strategy in the process was the development of team SMART goals and action plans. Teams were expected to monitor their data and goals on an ongoing basis. The team leaders led this charge with the principal's support in coordinating and helping them learn team, data, and goal-setting tools and skills. Time was provided for teams to work together.

This team approach is what Jenkins credits for the improvements Longfellow has made, both academically and behaviorally. For example, upon establishing the team approach, the discipline referrals to the office decreased notably. Because teachers were sharing expectations within their teams and talking about how to address behaviors that were not consistent with those expectations, they were able to manage discipline issues themselves. Additionally, as they monitored the data on behavior, they discovered an unusual trend, which ultimately became documented as a district-wide concern at the middle level. The trend they discovered was that regardless of whether discipline referrals decreased, the incidences of bullying and students' expressions of concern over bullying did not decrease. Now all of the middle schools in the district survey students on bullying and have programs in place to address student concerns.

In the realm of academics, the teams discovered that the Coulee school (one of the schools-within-a-school) was achieving noticeably better results in writing. Now that the teachers were accustomed to sharing across schools, their response to this difference was no longer a competitive one. Instead, they wanted to learn more. They asked, "How does Coulee get these results?" What they discovered was that Coulee's community-based approach required the students to conduct research within the community and to publish their writing on the Internet. For the students, this meant that their writing had to withstand public scrutiny; as a result, they were more careful about what they produced and were generally more aware of their writing. This "authentic performance assessment" served to improve writing overall.

Jenkins witnessed a transformation, not only of his school but within himself. He realized that for years he had been evaluating some teachers based on his opinions and attitudes about their teaching styles, philosophical approach, or even their personalities. When he examined the data, he realized that some of the teachers with whom he had struggled in the past were achieving some of the best results.

Continuous Improvement

Today, Longfellow Middle School continues to offer a wide variety of teaching and learning options for staff and students. Despite Jenkins' recent retirement, goal-oriented, data-driven improvement continues to be a high priority for Longfellow staff. Jenkins believes that now that staff have experienced the power of using data and goals to improve student performance, they will not go back to their old ways of doing things. They know for certain where they are experiencing the greatest success and now have the tools, skills, and processes for doing something about the areas in which they are not experiencing success. Each school has systems in place for monitoring and improving their own performance, but more importantly, an entire school system is in place for learning from each other. That's powerful!

"There are so many amazing things happening at Longfellow, it's hard to know where to start to sing their [staff, parents, and students] praises."

—Glen Jenkins

New Lexington High School, New Lexington, Ohio

How does a high school go from being on the state's "Needs Improvement" list to one of only 30 high schools in the state of Ohio to be recognized as a "School of Promise" within 2 years? Ask Dennis Love, Principal of New Lexington High School, and he will tell you, "It's really hard work! You have to go deep. You have to be focused. It takes time and hard work but if you want results, this process absolutely produces results!" The process Love speaks of is the SMART Schools 7-Step Problem-Solving Process. (For more information, see *The Handbook for SMART School Teams*, 2002, pages 195–203.)

We met Love and his "SMART Team" at a training session offered to 10 schools from across Ohio that had been identified as underachieving academically on state indicators. Funding and technical support for the training was provided by a grant from the Martha Holden-Jennings Foundation. The project, administered by Michaelene Meyer, the director of school improvement and professional development at Franklin County Educational Service Center in Columbus, was designed to bring best practices in instruction and school organization to underachieving schools committed to improving student results.

The training was voluntary and participation determined through a competitive application process. This put the training in a more positive light for the participating teams because they had been selected from among many interested applicants. The project was positioned from the start as an opportunity—not a punishment.

New Lexington High School brought a team of ninth-grade teachers representing each of the core subject areas, one sophomore social studies teacher, and the principal. The initial plan was that this "SMART Team," as they called themselves, would be the first to pilot what they were learning and that the entire staff would be brought on board in subsequent years. However, as the team began to look at their data and learn the school-wide SMART Schools process, they began to see the power of focusing the entire school on their greatest areas of need: reading and vocabulary development. New Lexington High School provides an excellent example of how an entire staff that is focused and committed to improving can demonstrate dramatic results in a short amount of time. This is their story.

"It is, and has been, the goal of the teachers and staff within all the buildings of the New Lexington City Schools to do whatever it takes to improve our schools for our children's sake. We want to develop and implement some new program(s) within the school to help our students perform better. Realizing that we have no funding with which to work, we need to look at the core of the problem and see how we can make the greatest change possible, working from the heart."

—New Lexington High School's *School Improvement Report*

New Lexington is centrally located within Perry County, Ohio, deep in the Appalachian Mountain region. At the 2000 Census, New Lexington lost its "city" status, falling from 5,117 inhabitants in 1990 to 4,689 in 2000. The population of the county, and New Lexington in general, is 98.7% Caucasian with

51.1% having attained a high school diploma as the highest level of education, 21.1% having not received a high school diploma, and only 2.4% having attained a master's degree or higher. The median household income is $34,383 with 25.9% making less than $19,000. Of the 9,414 families in the county, 885 (9.4%) are below poverty level.

The New Lexington City School District includes grades pre-K through 12. There are four schools in operation: elementary schools in both New Lexington and neighboring Junction City, a middle school, and high school (both in New Lexington). The district currently serves 1,898 students, 568 of whom are in the high school. For most regular academic classes, the average class ratio is approximately 25 students per teacher.

New Lexington High School, like the community of New Lexington, is largely agrarian with a low socioeconomic status. In the high school, 26.8% of students are "economically disadvantaged" and 14.4% are classified as "students with disabilities."

SMART Team Planning

The SMART Team moved full-steam ahead in their planning using QLD's 7-step "School Improvement Planning Process for Building SMART Schools," which incorporates the Plan-Do-Study-Act (PDSA) improvement cycle. What follows is the step-by-step documentation of their work.

Step one: Identify and define the student achievement problem. The team chose to focus their efforts on a school-wide issue, one that once corrected or amended, would benefit the most students. While analyzing test scores from past Ohio Proficiency Tests and practice Ohio Graduation Tests (OGT), the team uncovered a number of specific and individual areas of weakness. But one broader, more general area emerged as the one that could encompass and positively affect all the others: the acquisition of vocabulary. It is New Lexington's belief, as written in their *School Improvement Report*, that:

". . . students do not perform as well when they do not understand what is being asked of them and do not understand the terminology used in questioning. We are going to focus on raising students' acquisition of vocabulary in the hopes that it will correspondingly raise performance and achievement overall."

Step two: Analyze the problem. After careful analysis of test items, classroom vocabulary lists, and state standards and teaching practices, the team concluded that the problem with vocabulary may be occurring for a variety of reasons.

- Because of an inadequate supply of textbooks, teachers were providing instruction via notes and lectures. Students were required to enhance their learning of this new information by reading and researching on their own. This led to less consistent and less rigorous acquisition of the terminology than would have been possible if classrooms were adequately resourced.

- There was no systematic expectation or process for teachers to stress vocabulary development and assess the acquisition of vocabulary within their subject areas.

- There was no way of knowing whether students had learned the vocabulary on which they were being tested. It could be that they did not understand the vocabulary used in the test questions, in the instructions, and/or in the test response items.

- Students were not doing enough reading on their own, whether for pleasure or for the purposes of school, to have a good command of new words or of known words in different contexts.

- Since textbooks were not being issued to students in every class, the emphasis placed on reading and vocabulary development varied widely from classroom to classroom.

- Students did not understand how important building their vocabulary would be to their educations or lives.

Obviously, several of these issues were out of the control of the teachers, but that did not stop this SMART Team. The bottom line was this: If this process was going to produce positive results, the *students* needed to understand the importance of vocabulary in all aspects of their learning and they needed to understand the relationship between reading and success in life. Without a doubt, this had to be a school-wide endeavor across all subjects that was systematically implemented and assessed by all teachers.

Step three: Establish a specific goal for improvement. The following goal statement served as the foundation for the team's planning. Their goal was:

> "To implement a school-wide strategy that will strengthen the reading, speaking, and writing vocabularies of all students at New Lexington High School. The results will be measured using pre- and post-assessments developed by the staff and will also be measured by improvements in test scores on the reading, writing, and vocabulary portions of the Ohio Ninth Grade Proficiency Exam and the Ohio Graduation Test."

Steps four and five: Study and decide on solutions and strategies, and plan for implementation. After careful consideration of all the data and research on best practices in the goal area, the team identified two vocabulary-related strategies:

1. All teachers will make vocabulary a part of their weekly lessons.

2. A "word-of-the-day" program will be created and implemented school-wide.

Now the challenge would be to convince the rest of the staff that this was the right goal and that the strategies to be implemented on a school-wide basis were the best strategies to attain the goal. As one teacher said, "The most important part of this process and the most vital for its success and our survival was to implement the plan without a school-wide teacher stampede occurring." When asked what kind of resistance they met from the faculty, Love was quick to reply, "Not what you might expect." Because the staff had seen the data and had already been a part of studying possible solutions, they saw the need for a consistent research-based approach. Together they had read Marzano's *Classroom Instruction That Works* (2001) and Ruby Payne's *A Framework for Understanding Poverty* (1998), both of which pointed to vocabulary as a key success factor, especially for low SES students. The rationale for the change was clear; now it was up to the SMART Team to define the process for change.

Step six: Implementation. Beginning in January, each teacher provided the SMART Team with five vocabulary words from his or her content area that were taken from the glossary of the State Standards books. A vocabulary pre-test was compiled consisting of 25 words from the database. Teachers administered the pre-tests during their first period classes, graded them, and recorded the scores in an Excel spreadsheet. Reports compared students by grade level, by free- and reduced-lunch status, and by gender.

In February, the principal read a vocabulary word from the pre-test and its definition on the morning announcements. He did this every day for 5 days. Teachers wrote the word and its definition on a grease board in their rooms. After the 5 days, students took a 5-question multiple-choice quiz. Results were recorded as a grade in the students' first period class. An office aide recorded individual data in Excel. This process continued for approximately 5 weeks until all 25 words from the pre-test were used. After this, a post-test was administered to determine if acquisition of vocabulary had increased. They again compared students by grade level, free- and reduced-lunch status, and gender.

At this point the SMART Team developed a second pre-test made up of a new set of 25 words. The process of a word a day for 5 days continued for 5 weeks, at which point a second post-test was administered, results were recorded, and reports were made comparing the same data as before.

Step seven: Report results, analyze results, and draw conclusions. After analyzing the data, the team found that improvements were made in all categories. They discovered that the vocabulary acquisition gain was approximately two words. They found that females generally outscored males. By grade level, they found that all showed improvement ranging from one to three words. When examining students by free- and reduced-lunch category, both groups showed similar gains. The team discovered that the words chosen for round one were easier than round two and that the assessment was also not as difficult. So in developing round two questions, the team purposely created a more rigorous word list and incorporated better distracters on the multiple-choice questions.

Through these results, the group concluded that by providing daily vocabulary intervention all students were able to add to their vocabulary knowledge (figure 7.1). This process supports the idea that increased vocabulary acquisition will increase test scores on pre- and post-measures. The targets related to teacher-developed assessments were reached:

1. Gains were made from pre- to post-testing

2. All subgroups improved

But will this translate into improved performance on state tests? That was the team's original goal. The initial results look promising: from 2003 to 2004, reading proficiency increased from 59% to 74% and math proficiency increased from 26% to 48%. It is important to note here that just 2 years of data from

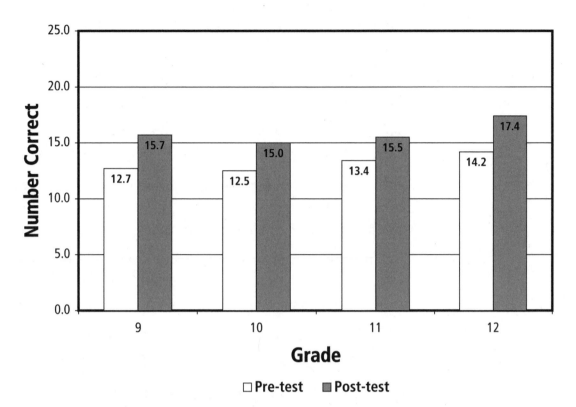

Figure 7.1: New Lexington High School Scores: Pre- and Post-test

two different groups of students does not give enough information to conclude that vocabulary development "caused" the increase. However, the combination of a focused approach with a very specific, consistent strategy for improvement clearly had a positive impact on this group of students.

After looking at all the results of their study, the team decided to continue with the same focus with some minor modifications to the implementation strategy. They decided to have the students become more involved by writing the vocabulary words in their notebooks.

Reflection

The SMART Team took some time to reflect, both collectively and individually, on what it meant to them to participate in the 7-step process. Here is what they found to be most useful:

- The process provided a logical order that allowed the team to stay on task.

- The steps kept the team focused on their goal.

- Step Three—Establish a Specific Goal for Improvement— helped the team define a goal that related directly to the purpose and the problem they were attempting to solve.

- By analyzing the problem at the level of root cause, the team could narrow its focus to an area that was most important for their students' success.

- Gathering additional data about the problem led the team to a deeper understanding of the problem, and therefore, to a deeper commitment to the solution.

- Linking the problem statements with verified causes helped them create the improvement goal.

The team also reflected on the challenges they faced. Not surprisingly, the most difficult part was finding time to work together as a team. What they discovered was that, because they did not have a designated, consistent time available to them, just finding time took time. Once they finally found the time to work together, they would have to back-track and review where they were in the process before they could move forward. This cost them even more time. Clearly, designated common planning time would be much more efficient.

For Principal Love, the SMART process has become a part of who he is as an educator. Not only has the process substantiated a set of life-long beliefs about the power of goals, data analysis, and collaborative problem solving, but it has also provided him and his staff with a blueprint for productive action. "What this has shown me is that with the SMART Team concept and a lot of input, we can accomplish great things. I truly believe that."

Based on the experience of the high school's team and the success of other participating New Lexington schools, the district has decided to make the SMART 7-Step Process a district-wide improvement strategy. Additionally, based on 3 years of results from the 10 districts that participated in the statewide project, the state and the foundation have agreed to continue to provide resources for the schools in the Jennings initiative to help share their successes with other Ohio schools "in need of improvement." The state is also developing the Jennings continuous improvement model into a school improvement framework that other schools in the state can implement.

"As I embarked on this journey, I was told this would help our students improve their scores on the Ohio Graduation Test. I was told that I needed to see the 'big picture.' I will admit that I did not see the big picture. I did not see it due to the frustration of being involved in different projects that did not seem cohesive. After months of being involved in this process, I am able to see the benefits of the SMART Team's efforts. The most satisfying part was seeing that it really can work. All of the work that we did can truly have a payoff. We need to keep our staff excited about this process, not overwhelmed. When we do this, everyone will see the 'big picture.'"

—Patty Wycinski, New Lexington Math Teacher

Burleigh Elementary School, Elmbrook, Wisconsin

SMART goals are at the center of learning for every teacher and student at Burleigh Elementary School in Elmbrook, Wisconsin. What began 8 years ago as a school improvement goal-setting and planning initiative has now become an integral part of every child's learning plan: SMART goals created and monitored by the students themselves.

Eleven years ago, Burleigh was the lowest performing school in the relatively affluent suburban school district of Elmbrook, located just west of Milwaukee. At that time, 20% of the students were performing below grade level. Today, in this school of 786 children,

90 to 96% of the students are demonstrating proficiency in reading, language arts, and math. Gains are evident throughout the school, but perhaps most notably in the area of special education. With 18% of the student population enrolled in special education, reading proficiency among special education students has increased from 39% to 63%; math proficiency has gone from 18% to 49%.

Burleigh did not begin its improvement process using SMART goals. That actually came many years after Principal Bil Zahn introduced the notion of shared governance to his staff. Teachers were invited to speak up, collaborate, and share decision-making about important instructional, assessment, and planning matters. Then, when the SMART goals process was introduced, it was seen as a logical continuation and deepening of the shared leadership model.

In the first year, the school's goals focused only on student behavior and discipline. In the second year, after staff had analyzed student achievement data from state tests and district assessments, it became clear that the goals needed to be more academic in focus. Improving reading and writing became the school-wide goal. Though gains in reading had already begun to show up when shared governance was implemented, when staff focused their goal-setting on reading and writing, they began to see more significant and more rapid achievement gains. Then in 2001 a former board member and parent of a Burleigh student suggested the idea of student involvement in the goal-setting process. That is when the next significant shift occurred. Burleigh's improvement strategy changed from a *school-based* model to a *student-based* model.

The Rest of the Story

Because staff had already begun to realize the benefits of shared governance and had already seen the positive effects of setting and monitoring SMART goals themselves, the shift was quite natural. Convinced that increasing students' responsibilities for their own learning would result in better achievement, the staff decided to give it a try.

Carol Commodore, the district's assessment coordinator, provided the faculty with research on student motivation, goal-setting, and student-involved assessment (Black & Wiliam, 1998; Wang, Haertel, & Walberg, 1994). Commodore conducted formal training in assessment *for* learning practices. The district's learning support coordinator, the reading specialist, and the instructional resource teacher provided student-friendly processes, templates, and tools to use with the students. The teachers took it one step further by translating SMART into kid-friendly terms: Specific, Measurable, Achievable, Real, and Timeline (O'Neill, 2004).

Support came in many forms. In addition to professional development provided by central office personnel, the staff participated in a variety of school teams designed to build their capacity to do this work.

- The School Improvement Leadership Team focused on school-wide support and planning.

- The Student Support Team focused on behavior.

- The Instructional Resource Team focused on instruction.

- The Burleigh Action Team (BAT) focused on policies and guidelines.

The teams were given time in the form of early release days once each week for collaboration and planning. Additionally, grade-level teams met weekly. Substitutes were brought in on an as-needed basis.

One of the keys to the success of this model is the way in which parents and all staff were included from the start. The Burleigh Action Team (BAT) is comprised of one representative from each grade level and department team, two parents at large, and two parents from the PTO. Custodians, secretaries, aides, specialists, students, and parents had ample opportunity to shape the goals and the strategies for achieving them. Everyone felt a part of the action; everyone shared responsibility for Burleigh's success.

When asked to reflect on their success, Principal Zahn points to three positive outcomes (O'Neill, 2004):

1. Students are more committed to trying harder to achieve their goals.

2. Students are more attentive to skill-based lessons designed to help them achieve their goals.

3. Teachers have better ways of assessing and providing feedback on student performance, are better at identifying individual students' skills and needs, and are more likely to provide an individualized approach to instruction.

According to Marge Willms, the instructional resource teacher at Burleigh, "Teachers are differentiating their instruction more. Students are selecting strategies using goal-setting worksheets that are directly tied to their individual SMART goals, and teachers are directing specific lessons to build those skills" (O'Neill, 2004, p. 37).

"What would it look like if part of our vision was that all students have input and ownership of their learning?"

—Bil Zahn (O'Neill, 2004, pp. 33–34)

The Path to Success

The stories in this chapter illustrate how SMART goals can be used in different ways to drive improvement. The context and culture of each school is different; therefore, each approach needed to be different. Not any one of these approaches will translate perfectly into your school environment, but collectively they will give you and your colleagues some ideas to consider, test, and discuss within your own learning communities. Then, the only thing left to do is to begin the journey. As it unfolds, another story will be told—yours.

Chapter 8

Renewing Our Schools, Our Practices, Ourselves

"The measure of success is not whether you have a tough problem to deal with, but whether it's the same problem you had last year."

—John Foster Dulles, Former Secretary of State

There is no question that teachers have one of the toughest jobs in the world. And the job isn't going to get any easier; in fact, in many ways it is getting harder. What other profession demands so much while simultaneously subjecting its members to such intense public scrutiny? What other profession asks its members to not only give of their skills and knowledge, but also so deeply of their hearts? And what other profession has the future of the world held so completely in its hands? The stakes are indeed high and the pressure intense, especially in today's world of global communications, accelerating scientific discoveries, deep environmental concerns, and world-wide conflicts. The students that are in our school systems today will need to be more resilient and flexible, more skilled in collaboration and reflective analysis, and more quickly adaptive to changing information than previous generations. Schools today, and the teachers who are face to face with students every day, are being presented with an interesting challenge: If we are going to help students for tomorrow, we will need the courage *today* to fundamentally change the way we have been "doing school." Many schools are developing both the will and the skill to make these changes, but others still have a long way to go. Why do we continue to keep doing what we have always done in the face of increasing challenges?

"Until you are willing to be confused about what you already know, what you know will never become wider, bigger or deeper."

—Dr. Milton Erickson, Psychiatrist, Psychologist, and Leading Practitioner of Medical Hypnosis

---

Let's look at an analogy: If you needed heart surgery, would you go to the surgeon who practiced in complete isolation, never read any new research, did not attend any professional development seminars, used the same techniques for 10 years, and then gave you reasons for why two out of five of his or her patients did not survive their surgery? Or would you seek out a surgeon who was in practice with other surgeons and met with these surgeons on a regular basis to review cases, attended conferences, kept up on the latest research, and was able to explain to you the innovative techniques he or she was using and the effectiveness of those techniques in increasing patients' longevity? Why does this choice seem to be a "no brainer" for healthcare while it is often such a difficult conversation in schools?

Fortunately many schools *are* fundamentally changing the way they operate. They are moving from isolationism to teamwork and shared leadership, from "doing our own thing" to a collective vision of what is important (and what is not), and from a "we teach, we test, we clean up the rest" philosophy to "we teach and assess, adjust and re-assess until each and every student can say, 'I get it.'" These schools are changing the conversation at every level to focus on improving student learning, using student learning as a filter for every decision: How will this help students learn? How will this help students learn *better*?

Teachers in these schools are courageously confronting whether they have both the skill and the will to make significant changes in their curricular, instructional, and assessment practices. They are stepping up to the plate to say, "I don't know how to do that but I'm willing to learn." These teachers are getting out of their classrooms to observe others' teaching and allowing others to come in and observe theirs. They are changing the way they think about curriculum from favorite units, textbook coverage, and/or teaching only what is on the test, to defining what is really essential and must be learned if students are to succeed. They are measuring whether as a result of their instruction students really are learning—each and every one—and they are willing to change if the evidence of learning is not there. These teachers are taking on leadership, risking their significance as they set SMART goals with their colleagues and their students, and pursuing these goals with all their hearts, souls, and collective wisdom.

Jan recently experienced this new model of teacher leadership first-hand as a parent. Her son Luke was experiencing great difficulty understanding fractions in fifth grade. Homework assignments ended in tears and he began saying he was "dumb" in math. After returning from a Canadian SMART Teams Institute where several participants had enthusiastically shared a web site for math, Jan downloaded a free curriculum from the site, and she and her husband arranged a conference with Luke's teachers who team together. The conference involved mutual problem-solving and open sharing. Luke's teachers said that they had seen a marked deterioration in confidence in their classes as a whole and had decided as a consequence to stop teaching fractions for a while. They explained that the district had requested that they try a new curriculum; based on weekly assessments of their students' understanding and on daily observations, they determined that the curriculum wasn't a good fit. They eagerly accepted the downloaded curriculum for review. Several months later Luke came home grinning. "Mom," he said, "the kids in my math class said to tell you, 'Thanks.' We get fractions now." Later he told a friend, "Fractions are my favorite subject." His classroom assessments and ability to complete homework on his own were clear evidence of his new understanding.

Team Reflection: Innovative Approaches

How do you learn about innovative approaches to instruction and curriculum? How do you test these innovations in your classrooms? How quickly can you find out how they're working for your students?

This story might not have had such a happy ending had Luke's teachers not had the courage to question the given curriculum, and then been open to trying a new approach.

Principals in these schools are changing the way they lead. They are letting go of the need to control each decision, and instead are deeply engaged in supporting each teacher in stepping up to leadership responsibilities themselves. They are creating systems and processes to support shared accountability, making sure that team conversations focus on improving student learning—setting and monitoring SMART goals, developing common measures to assess essential learning outcomes, researching and applying promising practices, and sharing what is being learned with other teachers in the school. They are courageously confronting mediocrity—if results are not being achieved, they are meeting with teachers to find out why, and offering support for change. If those teachers are not willing to change, they are moving them out of the classroom. These principals are learners themselves, constantly soliciting feedback about how they can improve as leaders, listening more than telling, and acting on what they hear. They are readers and reflective practitioners, building in time on a daily basis to reflect on their personal goals. They frame every conversation with "How can we . . . ?" and build on the strengths of the staff. They do whatever it takes to make sure teachers get what they need to help students get what *they* need to learn—regardless of politics and daily urgent "fires." They are visible and accessible, focused and engaged, hands-on and involved. But as capacity grows in the school, they know how to pull back, to allow the positive leadership energy of the group to take front stage, while they act more as "behind the scenes" facilitators and coaches. They are the lead cheerleaders for the school, finding and creating opportunities to celebrate progress and success, knowing that teaching is one of the most challenging professions in the world and that every teacher needs to know that what they are doing is helping kids learn.

"Schools with a strong normative environment focused on instructional goals promote a view of teaching as a body of skill and knowledge that can be learned and developed over time, rather than as an idiosyncratic and mysterious process that varies with each teacher."

—Richard Elmore (2000, p. 16)

Those of us who are passionate about being learners ourselves, who are never satisfied with the status quo, will constantly search for new and better ways to reach each and every student. Those of us who understand that the job is far too complex to be done alone will willingly collaborate with our colleagues to focus on SMART goals, develop ongoing assessments, and use those assessments to continuously improve our instruction and programs. And even if we have grown pessimistic over the years, having become convinced that nothing we can do will make a difference and that this focus on goals and feedback is just one more fad that will pass, we will become believers as we see others in our school experience the power of SMART goals to accelerate learning and improvement, and the excitement that they, their students, and parents express as they begin to see the results of their efforts. There will be a "tipping point"—that time where the school culture shifts from "we can't" to "we can and we will—together." As our schools grow collective intelligence through the SMART goals process, they will become places of true learning, where adults and children alike are sharing in the joy of coming to work and coming to school, knowing they have the power to make a difference.

References

Abplanalp, S. (2000). *An examination of the effectiveness of a professional development program designed to help teachers change the literacy program in an elementary school.* Madison, WI: University of Wisconsin.

Arter, J., & McTighe, J. (2001). *Scoring rubrics in the classroom.* Thousand Oaks, CA: Corwin Press.

Barth, P., Haycock, K., & Jackson, H. (Eds.) (1999). *Dispelling the myth: High poverty schools exceeding expectations* (Report No. SR9901). Washington, DC: Education Trust. (ERIC Document Reproduction Service No. ED 445 140)

Barth, R. (2001). Stepping back. *Journal of Staff Development, 22*(3), 38–41.

Black, P., & Wiliam, D. (1998). Inside the black box: Raising standards through classroom assessment. *Kappan, 80*(2), 139–148.

Buragas, A. (2004, May 25). Students narrow gaps in scores. *The Capital Times.* (Madison, WI), p. 1A.

Caine, R. N., & Caine, G. (1991). *Teaching and the human brain.* Alexandria, VA: Association for Supervision and Curriculum Development.

Calhoun, E. F. (2002). Action research for school improvement. *Educational Leadership, 59*(6), 18–24.

Calhoun, E. F., & Glickman, C. D. (1993, April). *Issues and dilemmas of action researching in the League of Professional Schools.* Paper presented at the Annual Meeting of the American Educational Research Association, Atlanta, GA.

Carroll, L. (2002). *Alice's adventures in wonderland and through the looking-glass.* New York: Random House.

Carstedt, G. (2004, October). *Shifting realities: Creating energy to revitalize organizations.* Keynote presentation at the Emerging Leaders Conference, Adelaide, South Australia.

Cawelti, G. (1999). *Portraits of six benchmark schools: Diverse approaches to improving student achievement.* Arlington, VA: Educational Research Service.

Collins, J. (2001). *Good to great.* New York: Harper Collins.

Combs, A. W., Miser, A. B., & Whitaker, K. S. (1999). *On becoming a school leader.* Alexandria, VA: Association for Supervision and Curriculum Development.

Commodore, C. A. (2001). *The impact of assessment on learners and their learning.* Ann Arbor, MI: Bell & Howell/ProQuest.

Conzemius, A., & O'Neill, J. (2001). *Building shared responsibility for student learning.* Alexandria, VA: Association for Supervision and Curriculum Development.

Conzemius, A. & O'Neill, J. (2002). *The handbook for SMART school teams.* Bloomington, IN: Solution Tree (formerly National Educational Service).

Covey, S. R. (1994). *First things first.* New York: Simon & Schuster.

Covington, M. V. (1992). *Making the grade: A self-worth perspective on motivation and school reform.* New York: Cambridge University Press.

Danielson, C. (1996). *Enhancing professional practice: A framework for teaching.* Alexandria, VA: Association for Supervision and Curriculum Development.

DuFour, R., & Eaker, R. (1998). *Professional learning communities at work.* Bloomington, IN: Solution Tree (formerly National Educational Service).

DuFour, R., DuFour R., Eaker, R., and Karhanek, G. (2004). *Whatever it takes.* Bloomington, IN: Solution Tree (formerly National Educational Service).

Dweck, C. S. (1999). *Self-theories: Their role in motivation, personality, and development.* Philadelphia: Psychology Press.

Easton, L. B. (2002). How the tuning protocol works. *Educational Leadership, 59*(6), 28–30.

Elmore, R. (2000). *Building a new structure for school leadership.* Washington, DC: Albert Shanker Institute.

Freiberg, H. J. (2002) Essential skills for new teachers. *Educational Leadership, 59*(6), 56–60.

Friedman, M. I., & Fisher, S. P. (1998). *Handbook on effective instructional strategies: Evidence for decision-making.* Columbia, SC: The Institute for Evidence-Based Decision Making in Education, Inc.

Fullan, M. G., & Stiegelbauer, S. (1991). *The new meaning of educational change.* New York: Teachers College Press.

Gardner, J. (1986). *The tasks of leadership.* Washington, DC: Independent Sector.

Glickman, C. D. (1993). *Renewing America's schools: A guide for school-based action.* San Francisco: Jossey-Bass.

Goleman, D. (1995). *Emotional intelligence.* New York: Bantam.

Goodlad, J. I., Klein, M. F., & Associates. (1970). *Behind the classroom door.* Worthington, OH: Charles A. Jones.

Gregory, V. H., & Nikas, J. R. (2005). *The learning communities guide to improving reading instruction.* Thousand Oaks, CA: Corwin Press.

Gregory, K., Cameron, C., & Davies, A. (2001). *Conferencing and reporting.* Merville, BC, Canada: Connections Publishing.

Grinder, M. (1977). *The science of nonverbal communication.* Battle Ground, WA: Michael Grinder & Associates.

Guskey, T. R. (2002). Does it make a difference? Evaluating professional development. *Educational Leadership, 59*(6), 45–51.

Guskey, T. R. (2003). What makes professional development effective? *Phi Delta Kappan, 84*(10), 748–750.

Hirsch, S. (2001). We're growing and changing. *Journal of Staff Development, 22*(3), 10–13.

Hobson, A. (1999). *From Everest to enlightenment: An adventure of the soul.* Calgary, AB, Canada: Inner Everest, Inc.

Holcomb, E. (1996). *Asking the right questions.* Thousand Oaks, CA: Corwin Press.

Jacobs, H. H. (2003). Connecting curriculum mapping and technology. *Curriculum/Technology Quarterly, 12*(3), 1–2, 4.

Jensen, E. (2000). *Brain-based learning.* San Diego: The Brain Store.

Johnson, D., & Rudolph, A. (2001). Critical issue: Beyond social promotion and retention—five strategies to help students succeed. Retrieved October 18, 2005, from the North Central Regional Educational Laboratory Web site: http://www.ncrel.org/sdrs/areas/issues/students/atrisk/at800.htm

Katzenbach, J. R., & Smith, K. D. (1993). *The wisdom of teams.* New York: Harper Business.

Kelleher, J. (2003). A model for assessment-driven professional development. *Phi Delta Kappan, 84*(10), 751–756.

Kendall, J. S., & Marzano. R. J. (2000). *Content knowledge: A compendium of standards and benchmarks for K–12 education* (3rd ed.). Alexandria, VA: Association for Supervision and Curriculum Development.

Killion, J. E. (2002). *Assessing impact: Evaluating staff development.* Oxford, OH: National Staff Development Council.

Lambert, L. (1998). *Building leadership capacity in schools.* Alexandria, VA: Association for Supervision and Curriculum Development.

Lambert, L. (2002) A framework for shared leadership. *Educational Leadership, 59*(8), 37–40.

Lambert, L. (2003). *Leadership capacity for lasting school improvement.* Alexandria, VA: Association for Supervision and Curriculum Development.

Langer, G. M., Colton, A. B., & Goff, L. S. (2003). *Collaborative analysis of student work: Improving teaching and learning.* Alexandria, VA: Association for Supervision and Curriculum Development.

Lewis, C. C., & Tsuchida, I. (1998). A lesson is like a swiftly flowing river: How research lessons improve Japanese education. *California Journal of Science Education, 4*(2), 12–17, 50–52.

Lezotte, L., & McKee, K. (2002). *Assembly required: A continuous school improvement system.* Okemos, MI: Effective Schools Products.

Little, J. W. (1993). Teachers' professional development in a climate of educational reform. *Educational Evaluation and Policy Analysis, 15*(2), 129–151.

Marshall, K. (2003). A principal looks back: Standards matter. *Phi Delta Kappan, 85*(2), 104–113.

Marzano, R. J. (2003). *What works in schools: Translating research into action.* Alexandria, VA: Association for Supervision and Curriculum Development.

Marzano, R., Pickering, D., & Pollock, J. (2001). *Classroom instruction that works.* Alexandria, VA: Association for Supervision and Curriculum Development.

McCarthy, B. (2000). *About learning.* Wauconda, IL: About Learning, Inc.

McKay, C. (2004, October). *SMART goal setting.* Presentation at Solution Tree's SMART Schools, SMART Teams Institute, Toronto, Ontario, Canada.

Moir, E., & Baron, W. (2002). Looking closely, every step of the way: Formative assessment helps to shape new professionals. *Journal of Staff Development, 23*(4), 54–56.

National Association of Secondary School Principals. (2004). *Breaking ranks II: Strategies for leading high school reform.* Reston, VA: Author.

National Staff Development Council. (2000). Monograph: Learning to lead, leading to learn. Oxford, OH: Author.

National Staff Development Council. (2001). *Standards for staff development*, revised. Oxford, OH: Author.

Newmann, F., & Wehlage, G. (1995). *Successful school restructuring.* Madison, WI: Center for Organization and Restructuring of Schools.

Newmann, F. M., & Associates. (1996). *Authentic achievement: Restructuring schools for intellectual quality.* San Francisco, CA: Jossey-Bass.

Newmann, F. M., King, M. B., & Youngs, P. (1999, April). *Professional development that addresses school capacity: Lessons from urban elementary schools.* Paper presented at the annual meeting of the American Educational Research Association, New Orleans, LA.

O'Neill, J. (2004). Teachers learn to set goals with students. *Journal for Staff Development, 25*(3), 32–37.

Payne, R. (1998). *A framework for understanding poverty.* Highlands, TX: aha! Process, Inc.

Perkins-Gough, D. (2003–2004). Creating a timely curriculum: A conversation with Heidi Hayes Jacobs. *Educational Leadership, 61*(4), 12–17.

Reeves, D. B. (2000). *Accountability in action.* Denver, CO: Center for Performance Assessment.

Rosenholz, S. J. (1991). *Teacher's workplace: The social organization of schools.* New York: Teachers College Press.

Sadler, D. R. (1989). Formative assessment and the design of instructional systems. *Instructional Science, 18*(2), 119–144.

Schmoker, M. (1999). *Results: The key to continuous school improvement* (2nd ed.). Alexandria, VA: Association for Supervision and Curriculum Development.

Senge, P. (1990). *The fifth discipline.* New York: Doubleday.

Sparks, D. (1999). The singular power of one goal: Action researcher narrows focus to broaden effectiveness. An interview with Emily Calhoun. *Journal of Staff Development, 20*(1), 54–58.

Sparks, D. (2001). Why change is so challenging for schools. An interview with Peter Senge. *Journal of Staff Development, 22*(3), 42–47.

Sparks, D. (2003). Honor the human heart: An interview with Parker Palmer. *Journal of Staff Development, 24*(3), 49–53.

Stiggins, R. J. (2001). *Student-involved classroom assessment* (3rd ed.). Columbus, OH: Merrill Prentice Hall.

Stiggins, R. J., Arter, J. A., Chappuis, J., & Chappuis, S. (2004). *Classroom assessment for student learning: Doing it right—using it well.* Portland, OR: Assessment Training Institute, Inc.

Wang, M. C., Haertel, G. D., & Walberg, H. J. (1994). Synthesis of research: What helps students learn? *Educational Leadership, 51*(4), 74–79.

Watanabe, T. (2002). Learning from Japanese lesson study. *Educational Leadership*, *59*(6), 36–39.

Wellman, B., & Lipton, L. (2004). Data-driven dialogue: A facilitator's guide to collaborative inquiry. Sherman, CT: MiraVia, LLC.

Whyte, D. (2004, June). *Cultivating the imagination*. Keynote delivered at the About Learning Renewal Conference, Chicago, IL.

Willis, S. (2002). Creating a knowledge base for teaching: A conversation with James Stigler. *Educational Leadership*, *59*(6), 6–11.

Wisconsin Taxpayers Alliance. (2004). Testing Wisconsin students. *The Wisconsin Taxpayer: A Monthly Review of Wisconsin Government, Taxes and Public Finance*, *72*(7), 1–11.

Make the Most of Your Professional Development Investment

Let Solution Tree (formerly National Educational Service) schedule time for you and your staff with leading practitioners in the areas of:

- **Professional Learning Communities** with Richard DuFour, Robert Eaker, Rebecca DuFour, and associates
- **Effective Schools** with associates of Larry Lezotte
- **Assessment *for* Learning** with Rick Stiggins and associates
- **Crisis Management and Response** with Cheri Lovre
- **Classroom Management** with Lee Canter and associates
- **Discipline With Dignity** with Richard Curwin and Allen Mendler
- **PASSport to Success** (parental involvement) with Vickie Burt
- **Peacemakers** (violence prevention) with Jeremy Shapiro

Additional presentations are available in the following areas:

- At-Risk Youth Issues
- Bullying Prevention/Teasing and Harassment
- Team Building and Collaborative Teams
- Data Collection and Analysis
- Embracing Diversity
- Literacy Development
- Motivating Techniques for Staff and Students

Solution Tree

304 West Kirkwood Avenue
Bloomington, IN 47404-5131
(812) 336-7700
(800) 733-6786 (toll-free)
FAX (812) 336-7790
e-mail: info@solution-tree.com
www.solution-tree.com

NEED MORE COPIES OR ADDITIONAL RESOURCES ON THIS TOPIC?

Need more copies of this book? Want your own copy? Need additional resources on this topic? If so, you can order additional materials by using this form or by calling us toll free at (800) 733-6786 or (812) 336-7700. Or you can order by FAX at (812) 336-7790, or visit our web site at www.solution-tree.com.

Title	Price*	Quantity	Total
The Power of SMART Goals	$24.95		
The Handbook for SMART School Teams	54.95		
Professional Learning Communities at Work	24.95		
Getting Started	19.95		
On Common Ground	29.95		
Whatever It Takes	24.95		
Assembly Required	34.00		
Classroom Assessment *for* Student Learning	58.00		
		SUBTOTAL	
		SHIPPING	
Continental U.S.: Please add 6% of order total. Outside continental U.S.: Please add 8% of order total.			
		HANDLING	
Continental U.S.: Please add $4. Outside continental U.S.: Please add $6.			
		TOTAL (U.S. funds)	

*Price subject to change without notice.

❑ Check enclosed   ❑ Purchase order enclosed
❑ Money order   ❑ VISA, MasterCard, Discover, or American Express (circle one)

Credit Card No._____ Exp. Date _____
Cardholder Signature _____

SHIP TO:
First Name_____ Last Name_____
Position _____
Institution Name_____
Address _____
City_____ State_____ ZIP _____
Phone_____ FAX _____
E-mail _____

Solution Tree (formerly National Educational Service)
304 West Kirkwood Avenue
Bloomington, IN 47404-5131
(812) 336-7700 • (800) 733-6786 (toll-free)
FAX (812) 336-7790
e-mail: orders@solution-tree.com • www.solution-tree.com

Solution Tree